PLAYBOYS AND KILLJOYS

BY THE AUTHOR

James Joyce: A Critical Introduction
(1941, 1960)

*The Overreacher: A Study of
Christopher Marlowe* (1952)

Contexts of Criticism (1957)

*The Power of Blackness: Hawthorne,
Poe, Melville* (1958)

The Question of Hamlet (1959)

*The Gates of Horn: A Study of Five
French Realists* (1963)

Refractions: Essays in Comparative Literature
(1966)

*The Myth of the Golden Age in the
Renaissance* (1969)

Grounds for Comparison (1972)

*Shakespeare and the Revolution of the Times:
Perspectives and Commentaries* (1976)

Memories of the Moderns (1980)

PLAYBOYS AND KILLJOYS

An Essay on the Theory and Practice of Comedy

HARRY LEVIN

New York   Oxford
OXFORD UNIVERSITY PRESS
1987

Oxford University Press

Oxford New York Toronto
Delhi Bombay Calcutta Madras Karachi
Petaling Jaya Singapore Hong Kong Tokyo
Nairobi Dar es Salaam Cape Town
Melbourne Auckland

and associated companies in
Beirut Berlin Ibadan Nicosia

Published by Oxford University Press, Inc.,
200 Madison Avenue, New York, New York 10016

Oxford is a registered trademark of Oxford University Press

LIBRARY OF CONGRESS CATALOGING-IN-PUBLICATION DATA
Levin, Harry, 1912–
Playboys and killjoys.
Includes index. 1. Comedy. 2. Dramatists. I. Title.
PN1922.L38 1987 809'.917 86-19190
ISBN 0-19-504856-3

9 8 7 6 5 4 3 2 1

Printed in the United States of America
on acid-free paper

FOR
RICHARD
AND
MARY ELLMANN

NOTE

The following pages originated in a series of lectures given at Oxford University under the Faculty of Mediaeval and Modern Languages during the Hilary Term of 1983, when I was the George Eastman Visiting Professor. Revised and abridged, they were delivered as Una's Lectures in the Humanities at the University of California (Berkeley) in March and April, 1985. In expressing warm gratitude to my sponsors and hosts, I should particularly mention Professor I. D. McFarlane of Oxford and Dean Donald Friedman of Berkeley. This published version incorporates a substantial amount of further revision and amplification. The interests it expresses have been on my mind through many years of teaching drama at Harvard University and occasionally writing about it. The late C. L. Barber, in his preface to *Shakespeare's Festive Comedy: A Study of Dramatic Form in Relation to Social Custom*, recalled the days when—as junior members of Harvard's Society of Fellows—we were both starting to think and talk about comedy. I also cherish lively recollections of later talks with my former student Erich Segal, when he was writing the doctoral dissertation that led to his *Roman Laughter: The Comedy of Plautus*. In bringing out my own book somewhat belatedly, I should like to recall those friendships and salute the valued contributions of those two good friends. A field of publication already large has meanwhile extended more widely, been canvassed by numerous bibliographies, and developed a kind of lingua franca among students of the subject. Where I have used terms or touched upon ideas from the ongoing discussion, I have tried to make specific acknowledgment through citations in context. However, I should single out two earlier works that I have found especially helpful and congenial: *Homo Ludens: A Study of the Play-Element in Culture* by Johan Huizinga and *The Fool: His Literary and Social History* by Enid Welsford. By way of supplement, I have reprinted four briefer essays which brought me to the present one. Though these have been slightly modified, there is still some overlapping, which at this stage may serve as links to reinforce the connection or to augment the documentation. My thanks to the copyright holders, then, for allowing me to reclaim this material: "From Play to Plays: The Folklore of Comedy" (originally presented as a Schweitzer Lecture in the Humanities at New York University, December 10, 1981), from *Comparative Drama*, Vol. 16, No. 2 (Summer 1982); "Notes toward a Definition of City Comedy," from *Renaissance Genres: Essays in Theory, History, and Interpretation*, edited by Barbara Lewalski, Harvard English Studies, XIII (Cambridge: Harvard University Press, 1986); "Introduction," from *Veins of Humor*, edited by Harry Levin, Harvard English Studies, III (Cambridge: Harvard University Press, 1972); and "The Wages of Satire," from *Literature and Society*, edited by Edward W. Said, Selected Papers from the English Institute, 1978, New Series, No. 3 (Baltimore: The Johns Hopkins University Press, 1980).

Cambridge, Massachusetts   H. L.
January 8, 1986

CONTENTS

PLAYBOYS AND KILLJOYS

POINTS OF DEPARTURE

It spoke unexpectedly well for the state of international literacy to note, prominent and recurrent on the list of recent best-sellers, Umberto Eco's *Name of the Rose* (*Il nome della rosa*). That lengthy, learned, and ingenious work of detective fiction is based upon a painstaking reconstruction of life in a medieval monastery. Readers who have pursued the story to its last revelation will have seen the mystery devolve upon a lost manuscript of Aristotle, an apocryphal sequel to his *Poetics*. Now the text of the *Poetics* as we have it, possibly an abstract or a transcription from lecture notes, is tantalizingly succinct. After some preliminary discussion of esthetic principles, it concentrates mainly on a thematic and structural analysis of tragedy and—in lesser detail—of epic. Comedy is merely touched upon by way of incidental contrast. The wish to see it treated more systematically has fathered the thought that there might have been a missing fragment. Such is what purports to be rediscovered in Signor Eco's novel, but only to be destroyed by the flames that ultimately consume his entire monastic establishment. The consummation is justified by his monkish pyromaniac on the grounds that, were this new source of Aristotelian wisdom to survive, it would provide a vindication of laughter, skepticism, and carnival.

Whether Aristotle himself would have fostered such genial notions, or whether—like many another serious thinker—he felt that comic levity deserved no more than a passing nod, lies beyond the scope of present conjecture. As the most encyclopedic of philosophers, he had briefly focussed his scientific curiosity on the matchless but necessarily limited phenomena of

Attic tragedy, through what proved to be the most influential of critical documents. It has been a problematic influence, as enforced by neo-classical scholiasts, who turned his empirical descriptions of Greek praxis into dogmatic prescriptions for later drama. Comedy, not having been so rigorously scrutinized, has never been so categorically schematized. Less subjected to preconceptions or rules, it has been less respectable, sometimes less than legitimate, and consequently freer to develop more widely and more diversely. Indeed its manifestations have been so widespread and so varied that they may discourage us from seeking a common denominator. We might find a word of encouragement in Ludwig Wittgenstein's dictum on games (a genus of which comedies are a species, as we shall be recognizing). We should look, he tells us, in *Philosophical Investigations*, not for a single formula but for a network of similarities, relationships, and family resemblances (*Familienähnlichkeiten*).

The conception of family likeness seems especially apt for the body of material we are approaching, since it brings out the dynastic continuity, the heritage of kinship, while duly allowing for the dissimilarities of individual talent and temporal adjustment. Tentatively we could trace our subject back, from an evolutionary or anthropological viewpoint, to a prehistoric origin in ritual and folklore. (Hesitating to begin so recessively, I have appended an article on protocomedy.) A live tradition, richly variegated and culturally interrelated, extends from the Old Comedy of Athens to the sitcom of television. One of comedy's premises is the persistence of types, as manifested in character, plot, and technical devices. This was virtually codified into standard casts and stock scenarios by the ancient and longstanding conventions of what—after more than two millennia—we still call New Comedy. These continued through the Commedia dell' Arte into, and well beyond, Molière; even Shakespeare was affected by them, in spite of his resistance to typology; and the movies fall back on some gags and gestures that were not novel when they were used by Aristophanes. However, we are entering a sphere where codes exist to be relaxed, and where surprises are all the more welcome because they break in upon sameness.

The corpus that we can draw upon, though it ranges all the way across Europe toward America, and from the classical to the contemporary era, may be viewed synoptically as an aggregate whole. To glance beyond it slightly would suggest that, where conventions differ, we can point to certain parallels, as with relatives in the Orient. The connecting link is the medium, the basic fact that comedies are written to be played upon a stage in the presence of an audience. Thus form is shaped by performance; the script is not fully realized until people interact with one another through a special bond of complicity; in a sense the playwright collaborates with the actors, who in their turn invite collaboration from the spectators. All of them are involved within a highly professional genre, which is just as much of a social institution as it is a literary art (and in another supplementary article I have tried to sketch its historic relationship with the culture of cities). So far as he can, a reader should restage the play in the theater of his mind, with imagination filling in the visual and vocal effects. When the comic repertory is gathered into the fold of literature, it retains a coherence and a concreteness which have been imparted to its texts by its theatrical contexts.

Through their peculiar closeness to the circumstances that produced them, comedies have registered the imprint of their times and places. Hence a tendency toward traditional uniformity is counteracted by shades of endemic difference. Devised to meet particular occasions, comedy outlives them by appealing to broad universals. The polemics of Aristophanes have outlasted a collective memory of the Peloponnesian Wars, and few of the many enjoying *The Beggar's Opera* have stopped to think about the peculations of Sir Robert Walpole. Hypocrisy in the name of religion is not yet a thing of the past, but it would be currently professed by other creeds than that of Molière's *faux-dévots*. Gogol's gibes against the Tsarist bureaucracy do not fizzle out for lack of targets in Soviet Russia. Literary ventures that aim at timeliness run the risk of obsolescence, and modern readers are understandably put off by outdated topical allusions which no array of footnotes could resuscitate. That is one reason why the enduring forest has been obscured so frequently by the ephemeral trees. There are other reasons—the sheer pleasure of resting in the shade or admiring the foliage or wandering down the by-paths—why the territory, for all the trudging through it, has never been very precisely or lucidly charted.

This does not mean that large outlines have not been pro-jected. On the contrary: "Comedy has provided a happy hunting-ground for the generalizers. . . ," according to L. C. Knights, whose own contributions have been more tangible. "Profitless generalizations are more frequent in criticism of comedy than in criticism of other forms of literature." Professor Knights's judg-ment, though severe, is incontrovertible, with regard to both the inordinate amount of free-wheeling speculation and its failure to enhance our critical understanding. Yet I suspect that there may be a clear explanation for that cloudy series of projections. Most of them are not addressed to comedy itself, under any kind of pragmatic definition, but rather to some immaterial essence vaguely classified as "the comic." The ambiguity is loose enough to encompass cause and effect, artistic constructs and states of mind. Interesting hypotheses from philosophy, psychology, and physiology are imposed upon literature a priori. Little or no distinction is drawn between genres, so that the relatively amor-phous novel often fits in better than the more tightly constructed drama. It is true, of course, that a number of pioneering novel-ists—Cervantes, Fielding, Stendhal—started out as dramatists; but their shift might well confirm the divergence between prose fiction and stage comedy.

If there were any single generalization that could be applied with equal relevance to Chaucer, Mark Twain, Evelyn Waugh, Milan Kundera, Milesian tales, Jewish jokes, banana peels, mech-anical toys, content analyses, laugh-counts, broadcasts, cartoons, monkeys, hyenas, and tickling, it would be much too sweeping for any plane but that of pointless platitude. Whatever could be said would hardly be worth saying, unless it took some account of the variances. I do not mean to limit consideration of certain attitudes and aptitudes that spread out into more than one mode of expression (and I shall try specifically, in two supplementary essays, to consider the conceptual linkages with humor and with satire). But comedy as such is so fruitful a field, so readily accessible and so concretely definable, that it claims centripetal attention. Critics today are much concerned, and justifiably so, with theories. We might agree that Anglo-American criticism, adept as it has become at interpretation and appreciation, has been laggard in conceptualization, in the comprehension of forms through ideas. It is therefore better versed in the products than in the processes of literature. Lately, amid the hurry and flurry of catching up, it appears to be pushing in the other direction; and theory, at too far a remove from the observable facts, can go astray.

That is where the comparative study of comedy offers its unique and available record of practice, which can be observed empirically and theorized about in more general terms. Its dramatic background, which has tested its practicality, could have likewise validated tragedy; but tragedy, on grounds that I have already indicated, has had a more sporadic and circumscribed history, while comedy has fallen heir to certain middling elements that had been excluded from tragedy. (Moreover, it would be snobbish and self-depriving to ignore non-literary comedy, whether in the cinema, the circus, the puppet-show, the nightclub, the music hall, or the opera house, so long as it is acted— or, for that matter, danced and sung.) Given the richness and the variety of the living models, it would serve no purpose to lay out skeletal composites. Though I shall be citing many playwrights and exemplifying from many plays—and hoping that some of the instances, mentioned in passing, might stimulate the reader's further interest to follow them up—this is not the place for detailed interpretation or rounded evaluation. Nor can it pretend to be a survey, chronological or systematic. We shall be proceeding by a synchronic method, letting the theoretical concepts frame the selection of practical examples, by their very nature a motley throng.

Seeking an appropriate level of discourse, somewhere between the spontaneity of a notebook and the regimentation of a treatise, I venture to present these observations as an essay. The inventor of that experimental form, Montaigne, could at least be called upon to license what might otherwise be regarded as an excess of quotations and illustrations, a density of reference elucidated by a discursiveness of style. In an area where speech is so important, there are some advantages in letting the principal interlocutors speak for themselves, whenever it seems pertinent—and sometimes, when they are foreigners, in their original language. Given the angles and latitudes of the subject, exposition tends to be more crab-like than strictly linear, with (in lieu of footnotes, which all too easily might have swamped the text) an occasional excursus or, at any rate, a parenthetical gloss. Arbitrarily but—I trust—expeditiously, the essay will be subdivided into twelve short sections, marking the successive stages of its argument. These will move back and forth freely, from long views to close-ups. Though the exemplification must be intermittent, dealing with the cases where the points arise, there should be a rough progression from the simple toward the complex. And it will be the strongest proof of the theory if, in its light, the practice is better understood and more thoroughly enjoyed.

1

COMING TO TERMS

Our subject is not as engaging as it might sound. Or rather, it has been so very engaging that—in order to enlarge our understanding of how it works—we must cultivate a certain disengagement. This, to be sure, is inherent in its workings, as Horace Walpole saw when he drew his familiar distinction: "The world is a comedy to those that think, a tragedy to those that feel." That distinction was shifted, in Charlie Chaplin's formula, from a psychological to a visual plane: "Comedy is life viewed from a distance; tragedy, life in a close-up." Classical commentators had regularly distinguished between tragic *pathos*, or emotion, and comic *ethos*, or conduct. The one entails involvement and the other detachment, though each presupposes its alternative to some degree. Romanticists could therefore sigh with Byron: "If I laugh . . . , / 'Tis that I may not weep." A wholly cerebral outlook, if it could be sustained for any length, would overrationalize or else gloss over feelings which had to be experienced in order to be fully apprehended. When we are teased, we ordinarily know that the taunts and threats will do us no harm. But to become detached is to have been attached, and that prior state of mind was less complicated.

Hence critics have had their troubles with comedy. Starting with the incidental allusions of Aristotle, it has proved "particularly unpropitious"—in Samuel Johnson's phrasing—to all except the sketchiest and most obvious definitions. The very richness and attractiveness of the material have tended to divert us from the course of critical analysis. We are understandably reluctant to see merrymaking reduced to a grim business. The present reversion of criticism to theory is, generally speaking, belated and long overdue, though we may seem to be reaching a point where the study of literature itself is getting overrun with theories rather less firmly grounded than Aristotle's or Johnson's. In the special case of comedy, as it has developed, there has been no lack of speculative discussion over the centuries. Yet here too the speculation seems to have outflown the practical conditions and the cultural forces that gave rise to the means of expression. That disembodiment has coincided with a departure from comedy's social matrix, the theater, in pursuit of an attribute known more abstractly as "the comic." As conceived so airily, in his lecture-essay on *The Comic Spirit*, George Meredith adumbrated some suggestive insights; but, like other eminent Victorians, he had little flair for or conversance with the stage.

Nor has much light been shed, from a more scientific standpoint, by isolating the phenomenon of laughter. Darwin has described its physiology and investigated its earliest stages in infantile behavior. Anthropologists have ascribed its bared teeth and facial contortions to the primitive display of snarling aggression and defense mechanism. Oscillographs have recorded its sound effects from the chuckle to the guffaw, the *sourire* to the *fou rire*; and volleys of cachinnation from studio audiences have been measured and rated by decibels. But, if it is a reflex, its fuller purport stays dependent upon the stimuli that evoke it— and tickling can produce the same result by the slightest manual stimulation. Nor are we appreciably wiser when we transpose a mixture of reactions, varying so widely from person to person and from culture to culture, into the conception of a single instinct which no experimental psychologist would acknowledge: namely, the sense of humor. In vivisecting laughs and anesthetizing laughers, gelastics proves to be a dismal science.

The contradictions of the philosophers in this matter, I believe, can be resolved by taking a more open and pluralistic view. Like the blind men with the fabled elephant, each of them has firmly grasped a different part of a large, complex, and peculiar creature. In groping toward a hypothesis, quite roughly, there have been two schools of thought. The first to be propounded, which emphasizes superiority (and thus connotes a bordering sphere of inferiority), stems from Hobbes's concept of "sudden glory": a subjective satisfaction with oneself over the infirmities or the misfortunes of others. For this unsympathetic attitude the Greeks had a word, *epichaírekakía*, more or less equivalent to the German *Schadenfreude*. A rough approximation in English would be "I'm all right, Jack, . . . !," with its unspoken corollary. That is why Plato, in his *Philebus*, disapproved of comedy. The second, which stresses incongruity (and thus connotes an implicit norm of congruence), derives from Kant's idea of a "strained expectation" that comes to nothing. This may be a more objective criterion, since it lies not in the eye of the perceiver but in the nature of the perception, in the object perceived and the strain of suspense leading up to an anticlimax.

Consequently I think that the two positions may be regarded as complementary, insofar as the first denotes a viewpoint and the second a situation. Briefly to take note of some further explanations: Freud, with his stress upon animus and release, falls into the first category, that of the beholder or laugher; whereas Bergson, with his emphasis on mechanism and reification, falls into the second, that of the beheld or laughingstock. Philosophy and psychology, in short, have been suggesting a theoretical basis for the dualism that runs through English criticism between wit and humor. Etymology is significant here. *Wit*, from an Anglo-Saxon keyword, is linked with the cogitations of the mind; *humor*, from a Latin medical term, with the fluids of the body;

and it was the unique role of Falstaff to bestride this complementarity. "I am not only witty in myself, but the cause that wit is in other men,"·he declares, and the latter disposition will elsewhere place him among Shakespeare's "irregular humorists." When humors were defined as eccentricities, "the humorous man" was a crank; gradually the humorist came to be seen as a person with an eye for such crotchets.

Now *ridicule*, the noun or verb in its etymological fullness, means laughing at (not with) somebody or something. I propose to call that vein of comedy *ridiculous*. But there is another source of risibility, or the capacity for laughter, which goes even deeper, and which should perhaps be accorded priority, since it involves a positive response rather than a negative judgment. This, as opposed to the satirical point or the rational purpose of derision, is the hearty laugh that—as Konrad Lorenz puts it—creates a bond. To share the fun with others is to play, whether in sheer frivolity or free experiment. That distinctive reaction can be summed up in the adjective *ludicrous*, which means "playsome," "sportive," "jocular," as differentiated from "ridiculous" by Lord Kames in an age when rationalism prevailed. Here the Latin root-word *ludus* has the same double meaning as the English *play*, both game and drama, and likewise as the French *jeu* and the German *Spiel*. Blurred together, *ludicrous* and *ridiculous* seem to have become loosely synonymous, but I should like to reaffirm the distinguishing nuance, as it was well understood by the Scottish rhetoricians. Though our problems will not be solved by coining new terms, we may find it illuminating now and then to reexamine some of the terminology that has figured in earlier discussions.

A discerning historian, Johan Huizinga, wrote a stimulating book to show how much the textures of civilization owe to the activities of *homo ludens*, man at play. Man deluding, *homo deludens*, would cross over from the ludicrous to the ridiculous, as we should be seeing by and by. Moreover, he can collude as well as delude: an actor, notably, counts upon the *collusion* of his audience. Together they take reciprocal parts in creating an *illu-*

sion, converging just beyond the edge of everyday reality, and waking from their fantasies of escape to the anxieties of *disillusionment*. No wonder they so often ask themselves—like Master Ford, about to cuckold himself in *The Merry Wives of Windsor*— "Is this a vision? Is this a dream? Do I sleep?" Such a confusion is typical of the comic protagonist. Whether he is bemused by revery or bewitched by magic, intoxicated by drink or hallucinated by drugs, being deceived or deceiving himself or simply going crazy, he must face an eventual awakening—happily if he has been undergoing a nightmare, sadly if he has been enjoying a wishdream. Though we shall not be moving in high altitudes, dizziness will be a common complaint.

The quality that imagination suffuses through the arts is essentially that of a waking dream. Though playfulness is a distraction and a diversion—distraction from the duties of ordinary life, diversion from the routines of regular employment—it observes conventions of its own. Many a game has survived by going through motions that began as rituals: Mother Goose's collection is full of fossilized examples, surviving fragments of protocomedy. The art of gamesmanship is manifested in gambling as well as gamboling; and the players are gamesters, engaged in games of chance as well as skill. Though they are no less eager to be surprised by bountiful fortunes than loth to be overwhelmed by adverse contingencies, the outcome that they hazard is aleatory, whereas for tragic figures it seems fatally predestined. When "the sport" was particularized with the definite article, it conveyed a sexual connotation on the Restoration stage. "We hunt in couples," says the hero to the heroine of Congreve's *Double Dealer*, "both pursue the same game." And later on the two agree that "Marriage is the game at which we hunt."

Bearing in mind this basic antithesis, we shall be engaged throughout in tracing a dialectical interplay between the ludicrous and the ridiculous. But first it should be set against the primary context of a broader dichotomy: the relation between comedy and tragedy. Socrates argued, it will be recollected, that the same genius would be adept at both genres; however, *The*

Symposium tapered off in vinous slumbers soon afterward, before he could explain his reasoning; and it remained for Shakespeare's works to demonstrate what, for Plato, must have been a barely conceivable paradox. This might cast a sidelight on why Shakespeare has been so hard to pin down, particularly under the aspect of comedy. Comedy and tragedy: the whole range of human experience in all its complexity can be stylized and symbolized but scarcely encompassed by that pair of complementary masks, that choice of grins or frowns, that polarity of *L'Allegro* and *Il Pensero*. By pointing out how incomplete and arbitrary it was, Dr. Johnson was able to rescue Shakespeare from the cavils of neo-classicism.

The generic dividing line, even with Shakespeare, had never been based on the use of prose or verse. Comedy, more readily than tragedy, has been attuned to colloquial speech; but, since it has been more preoccupied with love, it has also produced its own lyricism, musically as well as stylistically. Its intrinsic playfulness has luxuriated in language: puns and nicknames, dialects and inventories, epigrams and wisecracks, badinage and persiflage, blandishment and vituperation, euphuism and malapropism. The linguistic dexterity of Aristophanes' choruses reached its uproarious climax in a *pnigos*, or tongue-twister. Shakespearean drama abounds in silver-tongued set-pieces: Jaques' blank-verse monologue on the seven ages of man is mockingly countered by Touchstone's prosy disquisition on the seven causes for quarreling. Molière's characters underline his themes when they reiterate their *mots de caractère*, as in his bourgeois gentleman's insistence that everything be fit for "*les gens de qualité*" or his miser's delight in withholding a daughter's dowry: "*sans dot.*" Corporal Nym speaks for comedy in general with his watchword: "And that's the humor of it."

If tragedy elicits our compassion, comedy appeals to our self-interest. The former confronts life's failures with noble fortitude, the latter seeks to circumvent them with shrewd nonchalance. The one leaves us momentarily in a mood of resignation, the other in a condition of euphoria. But there must be additional possibilities. Even the Greeks seem to have recognized a third dramatic genre in the satyr play, which seems to have been a sort of mythological burlesque—to judge from the surviving *Cyclops* of Euripides, whose tragedies verged episodically upon the borders of comedy. By and large, it was comedy that provided the more flexible form, so that in Spanish the word *comedia* signified almost any kind of play, just as the word for "comedian" signifies any actor in several other languages than English. Happy endings are unreliable tests, so long as Dante's apocalypse is classified as a comedy, or the *Philoctetes* of Sophocles as a tragedy. Yet even where the Hellenic patterns have not been imprinted, modes have been contrasted within the repertories of drama. For instance, between performances of the classic Noh in Japan, farces were interpolated, the *kyōgen*. The contrast between heroic idealization and a tendency toward caricature seems well-nigh universal, though outsiders may not always sense the peculiarities of a given esthetic idiom.

Above all, there remains a crucial difference between the vicarious sympathy that identifies an observer with a protagonist and the sharpened observation that detaches them from each other, which may be attributed to a widening of perspectives. The uniqueness of the tragic protagonist is marked by superlatives. Titus Andronicus views himself as "The woefull'st man that ever liv'd in Rome." And virtually every tragical lover is a nonpareil: "For never was a story of more woe / Than this of Juliet and her Romeo." But when Rosalind tries to cool Orlando's ardor in *As You Like It*, she enumerates a series of mythical exemplars who neutralize the tragic potentialities into a comic generalization: "Men have died from time to time and worms have eaten them, but not for love." If a lover is saying farewell to his sweetheart and going off to war, we may well sympathize with them both and join in their mutual commiseration. But if these lovers are saying farewell on stage right, and if a similar couple is doing the same on stage left, and if all four are dancing and singing—along with their mentor—what turns out to be a quintet with music by Mozart, then we have grounds for noting and generalizing: "*Cosí fan tutte*, they'll do it every time, that's the way all women behave, it's the way of the world."

Modern playwrights, exempt from conforming to the ancient models, nonetheless felt some need to discriminate, as Bernard Shaw did when he entitled his early two-volume collection *Plays Pleasant and Unpleasant*, or Jean Anouilh when he separately published *Pièces roses* and *Pièces noires*. Comedy and tragedy both sprang from parallel, if not identical, origins—insofar as the classicists have been able to explore them, from sacrificial feasts and other religious ceremonies. Each rite had its myth in due season, and the play-acting formed part of the celebration. To his tutelary altar in the orchestra, that dancing-place of the original Greek theater, Dionysus, the ecstatic god, brought with him the choric adjuncts of wine, women, and song in early spring. Comedy has been traced back to the revel, or *kōmos*, which in turn looks ahead to the Aristophanic finale, the wedding or *gamos*. Phallephoric processions, orgiastic dances featuring satyrs rather than heroes, were a comic counterpart to the stately tragic dithyrambs, which had fostered panegyric rather than invective.

Revelry—licensed disorder, sometimes proclaimed by obscenities—was the scheduled order of the day; and the date was perforce a holiday, as it would be with the Saturnalia in Rome, and with the analogous seasons of carnival in other cultures, when the conventional observances of society were relaxed and even reversed for a topsy-turvy interim. Normally the rules would be reaffirmed by the episodes of misrule—though Leroy La Durie, in his *Carnival at Ornans*, has documented one such occasion when the subversion ended by overturning the status quo. "Come, woo me, woo me," says Rosalind to Orlando, thereby reversing the protocol of the sexes, "for now I am in a holiday humor, and like enough to consent." It is that holiday humor which pervades the atmosphere of Shakespearean comedy from Midsummer Eve to Twelfth Night, from the vernal sheep-shearing festivities in *The Winter's Tale* to the autumnal harvest rites in *The Tempest*. Even when the appointed day does not celebrate a ceremonial occasion, it becomes—with all its programmed outbursts of spontaneity—a happening, a heyday, a field day, a May Day, an April Fools' Day.

Comedy benefits from being crowded, struggling and kicking, into the Aristotelian span of one natural day—or better still, a night: "That Night," as the silent screens used to announce so climactically. We should remember that Goldsmith's *She Stoops to Conquer* is subtitled *The Mistakes of a Night*; nor, since titles are the most conspicuous signifiers, should we forget that *Le Mariage de Figaro* is merely Beaumarchais' subtitle for the play he called *La Folle Journée*. The Marx Brothers managed to combine this diurnal or nocturnal timing with a recreational background designed to make the most of it: *A Day at the Races*, *A Night at the Opera*. It remained for the Beatles to compound *A Hard Day's Night*. "If all the year were playing holidays," soliloquizes the Prince in *Henry IV*, "To sport would be as tedious as to work." All play and no work would make Hal a silly boy. If a holiday is to be really enjoyed, it should be a day off, a day out, *A Day in the Country*, a rare spell of liberation from workaday chores. *Homo ludens*, after all, is *homo laborans* on vacation; the pastimes of his leisure (*otium*) afford him relaxation from the responsibilities of his business (*negotium*).

When the Menaechmus of Epidamnus, the hard-working, stay-at-home twin brother, is goaded by domestic frustrations into taking a night out, the Parasite asks him what's up and he answers: "*Furtum, scortum, prandium*"—a threefold regimen of exemplary riotous living. We might catch something of the succinct Plautine jingle with "Pinching, wenching, lunching." It heralds a major comic gambit, the escapade, which juxtaposes two contrary lifestyles, that which we escape from and that which we escape to. To appreciate ludicrousness, William Hazlitt admonished, in his genial essay on "Wit and Humour," one must be aware of seriousness. Carnival would be warranted by Lent. Comedy has often braved the indifference, and sometimes risked the disapproval, of those who are not amused, those who are never likely to be amused, whom Meredith—borrowing a coinage from Rabelais—christened the agelasts, the non-laughers.

Their patroness should have been Mrs. Grundy, a character in Thomas Morton's once-popular melodrama, *Speed the Plough*, whose offstage presence continually shamed the other characters into wondering what she would think or say about their goings-on. Accordingly, she came to personify the standards of Victorian respectability that Oscar Wilde would mock in *The Importance of Being Ernest*.

Wilde, for whom art was "the only serious thing in the world," characterized that play, in one of those verbal polarities which set its tone, as "a trivial comedy for serious people." For both of his heroines, as for Longfellow, "Life is earnest." The light-minded Jack does not become a solid citizen by changing his name to Ernest; nor does his friend, the aphoristic Algy, who is "never serious." But their holidays incognito—like Lady Windermere's past, like Dorian Gray's portrait—hint furtively at Wilde's own secret escapades, which were so soon to provoke Mrs. Grundy's public revenge. Wilde strung his epigrams on an improbable plot, farcical rather than melodramatic as in his other and lesser plays, refining upon the recent success of the giddy *Charley's Aunt*, yet harking back to the prototypes of Terence. Accordingly, the ex-governess Miss Prism plays the Nutrix, the absent-minded nanny who turns up so conveniently to complete the recognition of the long-lost orphan, and thereby to legitimatize the out-of-hand predicament. Yet in what timely purlieu did she lose her identifying handbag? Where else but in Victoria Station?

2

RULES OF
THE GAME

Thus comedy recycles the oldest devices. The Savoy Operas constitute a veritable museum of histrionic conventions. Bernard Shaw updates the stock formulas by turning them upside down. The juvenile twins of *You Never Can Tell*, though brought up on twentieth-century treatises (predated in 1897), masquerade as Harlequin and Columbine, and turn the last act into a transformation scene from a Christmas pantomime. In Shaw's first play, *Widowers' Houses*, it is the lovers who perversely raise financial complications when their parents rashly want to see them married; and it is the complicating factor, the slumlord issue, that strikes the "unpleasant" Shavian note. As Shaw confessed elsewhere, repeating Wilde's shibboleth, "the real joke is that I am in earnest." Wilde, on the other hand, had called for a "New Hedonism," and had presented characters—like Viscount Goring in *An Ideal Husband*—who seem to be "living entirely for pleasure" (or like Lady Hanbury in *The Importance of Being Ernest*, when her husband died and her hair "turned quite gold from grief"). This does not sound quite so natural as the old hedonism of Rabelais: the "Do what thou wilt [*Fay ce que vouldras*]" of his Abbaie de Thélème.

The latter-day cult of the pleasure principle, for better and for worse, would not be as single-minded as that of the Restoration, when Mistress Lovewit resolved, in Etherege's *Man of Mode*: "We'll sacrifice all for our diversion," and Pinchwife told Horner, in Wycherley's *Country Wife*, "Your business is pleasure." Hymning the praise of free love in the Renaissance, Tasso's *Aminta* had dared to affirm that whatever pleased was permitted: "*se piace è lice*." But that would have been in some Arcadian Golden Age, or else—as Charles Lamb characterized it, with his apologia for the Restoration dramatists—"a Utopia of gallantry." In the theater, nonetheless, to please (*plaire*) is "the great rule of all rules [*la grande règle de toutes les règles*]," laid down by Molière himself in *La Critique de l'École des femmes*. All the other rules prescribed by the academic authorities are either negligible or nonexistent, as successful playwrights have attested from Lope de Vega to George Farquhar. "The drama's laws the drama's patrons give," as Johnson's prologue declared at the opening of Garrick's Drury Lane, and the axiom was followed by a play upon words which wryly accepts the necessities of show-business: "For we that live to please must please to live."

Every epilogue, in its own way, repeats what Feste the jester sang for the tag-line of *Twelfth Night*: "And we'll strive to please you every day." The farewell appeal for applause in Latin comedy, as Northrop Frye reminds us, brought the playgoers into the play's resolution: "*Plaudite, spectatores, et valete.*" But they have been participants all along: when Aristophanes warned them to look out for the dung-beetle overhead, when the Plautine stage-manager offered them free advice, when Peter Pan begged them to suspend their disbelief in fairies, when Molière's plundered miser Harpagon inquired of the *parterre*: "*Messieurs, mon voleur, n'est-il point caché là parmi vous?*"—and the implication was an accusation, implying that the audience harbored thieves. Molière was criticized for breaking the spell of naturalistic illusion, whereas he was actually reinforcing an older spell of audience participation, while closely imitating the desperate outcry of the miser Euclio in Plautus' *Aulularia*. When the puppet Guignol voices a similar query today, the attending French children will loudly answer and obligingly point in the direction taken by the thief.

Theorists have not acknowledged, until quite lately, the extent to which the spectator shares in the spectacle. It may have embarrassed their residual earnestness to concede that so much energy had been spent in a mutual process of amusement. Revelling is both unrespectable and disrespectful by nature. Hence much less attention has been paid to the ludic and festive than to the didactic and satirical. Horace, characteristically attracted to the mean between alternatives, balanced the useful against the agreeable (*"utile dulci"*) and profit against delight (*"aut prodesse aut delectare"*). The equivocation of that *either/or* prompted classical critics to overstress the ethical component. When Bergson specifies playthings as laugh-provoking mechanisms, we should be more mindful than we ordinarily are of his protective concern for the underlying concept of organic vitalism. Meredith sought to rest his case on "the uses of comedy." It was a just trial, nothing less than a critique of civilization, for the Earl of Shaftesbury, who considered ridicule to be the test of truth. Aristophanes would never have passed that test; for his targets—apart from the tragedy of Euripides, whose reputation thrived upon the publicity—included the demagogy of Cleon and the sophistry of Socrates; and, while Cleon went undamaged by the attack, alas, Socrates did not.

Truth was not vindicated in either case. Nor has comedy managed to serve a utilitarian function, in spite of those Irish bards who claimed that their verses could exterminate rats. Many diatribes and apologetics have been devoted to its moral impact pro and contra, inasmuch as enemies of drama—from the Church Fathers on—have focussed upon its frivolous surfaces and its hedonistic implications. Vainly the apologists have attempted to meet the moralists upon their own ground, as in the controversy wherein Congreve joined issue with the puritanical Jeremy Collier. To argue that comedy could reform and elevate was to assume that it influenced conduct one way or another, and consequently to admit that it could deprave and corrupt just as easily. Its proponents justified it as a social corrective. It should be, according to Sir Philip Sidney, "an imitation of the common errors of our life, which [the poet] representeth in the most scornful sort that may be, so as it is impossible that any beholder can be content to be such a one." The premise of Ben Jonson's "comical satire" was that the spectators, recognizing their faults and foibles, would improve their behavior. Caught up in a rearguard action against the uncompromising Puritans, Sidney and Jonson both conceived the drama as an object-lesson, a cautionary fable.

So did their contemporary, Pierre de Larivey, the pioneering writer of French comedies, using the standard metaphor for a projected image (*"le miroir de notre vie"*): "Comedy being the mirror of our lives, old men learn to keep from looking like dotards, young men to control themselves in love, ladies to safeguard their virtue, and fathers and mothers to take care of their families." If a playwright dwells upon errors or pitfalls, presumably it is because he would teach us to avoid them. Larivey's exemplars—elders, youths, lady-loves, parents—were inevitably those who had been incorporated into Greco-Roman tradition. They were enshrined in the works of Terence, which had conveyed their comic paradigms through the Middle Ages, but scarcely the *vis comica* itself; for his original audiences had not found them amusing in performance; and his defensive prologues bear witness to their relative unpopularity. He survived as a sententious pedagogue. When he is revived at Westminster School each Christmas, as he was in the schooldays of Jonson and Dryden there, it is because the Elizabethan statutes recommended him as a model of counsel (*"concilium"*) and good style (*"bene loquendi"*). Whenever a *sententia* comes up, one of those schoolboy maxims for which he was so much quoted, the youthful performer steps forward and addresses himself to his fellow students, who have been instructed to applaud.

Professionals might well protest, with Sheridan, that the Comic Muse was happiest in the dazzle of the footlights, which reminded her of what the drama's patrons expected. Pointing to her effigy on one side of the Covent Garden stage, the Prologue to *The Rivals* wondered rhetorically:

> —Look on her well—does she seem form'd to teach?
> Should you expect to hear the Lady—preach?

Yet she could disarm suspicions, meet criticisms, and at times take shelter within the academy, by professing herself an exponent of wisdom, conventional as well as unconventional. As such, she came to terms with the morality play, the *auto sacramental*, the masque, the *pièce à thèse*, agitprop, and other dramatic vehicles for ideas and ideologies. The idea could be as commonplace as a proverb or proverbial phrase: *You Never Can Tell, You Can't Take It with You*—comic admonitions both, one predicting surprise, the other prescribing enjoyment. It could lead the Elizabethans to dramatize some rather well-worn adages: *Hot Anger Soon Cold, The Weakest Goeth to the Wall, Enough is as Good as a Feast, All's Well That Ends Well.* Shakespeare's title is somewhat less distinctive than these others, since it would have fitted any of his comedies, with the possible exception of *Love's Labor's Lost.* Since this applies to any imbroglio that finds a solution, it could hardly be more general—or more germane to comedy.

Calderón could deliberately set out to illustrate the notion that a house with two doors is hard to watch (*Casa con dos puertos mal a se de guardar*), Pirandello to ironize the assumption that things are what they seem (*Così è, se vi para*). Carmontelle, who established the minor dramatic genre based on proverbs in the eighteenth century, explained that "there is no comedy which could not be given a proverb for a title." This simplistic mode is best remembered through the *Proverbes* of Alfred de Musset, those gallant conversations which—like charades—move through a drawing room toward the fulfilment of their titular dictum: *On ne badine pas avec l'amour, On ne saurait penser à tout, Il ne faut jurer de rien.* Most of Musset's precepts seem to be negations, with a shrug or a warning—no trifling with love, not thinking of everything, not swearing to anything. Seldom could a moral be so briskly imposed upon a situation or so expressly pushed toward its conclusion. Yet something like it was implied by one of our recurrent figures of speech: the Ciceronian *"speculum consuetudinis"* (or "glass of custom"), the Shakespearean mirror held "up to nature," which in their respective turns have restated the Aristotelian "imitation of life."

Where the reflection flashes a message, it is supposed to act as an aid to self-correction. When a realistic looking-glass is set before an observer, it is assumed that—upon due observation—he may wish to mend his ways, or at least that she may start to primp a little, as the quotation from Larivey suggests. The resemblance can be ignored by the incorrigible, or passed off as merely coincidental by the thick-skinned. But, as the motto to *Revizor* advises: "Don't blame the mirror, if there's something wrong with your face." Gogol dramatizes that epigraph when, after the pecadillos of a small-town bureaucracy have been thoroughly exposed, the Mayor turns and taunts the hilarious spectators: "What are you laughing at? Yourselves." Then a *tableau vivant*, into which the actors freeze, holds up a mirror-image to the audience. This exposure has been precipitated after Hlestakov, an insignificant but insouciant clerk from a government office, has been mistaken for the important Inspector General, and consequently welcomed and placated with hospitality and bribery. In the comparable satire of Carl Zuckmayer, *Der Hauptmann von Köpenick*, a wily cobbler hoodwinks and browbeats the local officials by dressing up in an officer's uniform. His imposture—effectual while it lasts—is deliberate, whereas Hlestakov's was accidental, an assumed identity depending on the mistakes of others rather than native guile.

Consider another case of inadvertent initiation, where a feckless stranger is complacently feted by a provincial community on the basis of a misunderstanding about who he happens to be, J. M. Synge's *Playboy of the Western World*. Christy Mahon owes his hero-worshipping reception to a highly exaggerated rumor of parricide. Despite the resurrection of his father, it is a rite of passage for the long-repressed son—possibly, one might add, a symbolic gesture of Irish rebellion against British rule and, more universally, a psychic deliverance from constraining authority. The play takes place in what might be a broken-down Dionysiac shrine, actually a rustic shebeen "near the wild coast of County Mayo," and proceeds from a wake to a feast, with concomitant sports and games wherein the anti-hero triumphs. The free play of this Western World reflects a different image of himself from the familiar one with which Christy grew up. "Didn't I know rightly I was handsome," he now exults, "though it was the divil's own mirror we had beyond, would twist a squint across an angel's brow."

The worm has turned, the ineffectual plodder has blossomed out, not as an angel but as a playboy, straying after Dionysus and his wayward crew, junketing down the highway to Gadshill with Falstaff, joining the escapades of Wilde's men about town, "going on a spree" in the formula of Johann Nestroy's *Einen Jux will er sich machen*. The well-tried efficacy of that formula has been tested by Nestroy's Viennese adaptation from an earlier English farce by John Oxenford, *A Day Well Spent*, and by its readaptation into English through Thornton Wilder's *Merchant of Yonkers*, more successfully reworked as *The Matchmaker*, and ultimately set to music and filmed as *Hello, Dolly!* (Tom Stoppard has recently added to the chain with *On the Razzle*, a closer rendering of the Nestroy version.) Playboys all, the games these anti-heroes play may appear to be childish or outmoded, silly or shady, but they are fundamentally celebrations, working days giving way to holidays. Having been set in motion—so Falstaff expressed it—"for recreation sake," they conduce to a state of refreshment, if not rejuvenation. Literally, *The Knights* of Aristophanes culminated in a ritual bath, which restored the youth of the citizen Demos.

The care and preservation of human life depend upon such

playful relaxations, which had the sanction of Saint Thomas Aquinas: *"Ludus est necessarius ad conservationem humanae vitae."* The Banns of the *Ludus Coventriae*, introducing the most professionalized sequence of English mystery plays, promised:

> Whan that ye can, there shal ye sene
> The game well played, in good aray.
> Of holy wrytte this game shal bene,
> And of no fablys be no way.

The very truths of Scripture, not pagan fictions, could be played like a game. Shepherds, awaiting the Nativity, took part in rural sports; choirboys, on certain occasions, burlesqued the liturgy; and schoolmen indulged in sessions of misrule. Yet misrule has never prevailed without generating its own regulations, mimicking while subverting the established regimen. To please may be the greatest of all rules, but most games have their little rules of thumb. It has been the part of convention to take them for granted, but modern dramaturgy has become increasingly conscious of itself and of life's theatricality. Luigi Pirandello exemplifies this reflexive awareness, perhaps most strikingly in *Il giuoco delle parti*—the phrase enfolds so many of those ambiguities that it has been freely translated as *Rules of the Game*, though its literal signification is both a game and a joke, and its men and women are merely role-playing. Though it is less well known than *Sei personaggi in cerca d'autore*, scenes from it are rehearsed therein as the play-within-the-play. Here one game leads to another: marriage to adultery, and adultery to a duel, where the final joke is on the would-be joker.

There is an abortive duel and an authentic murder in Jean Renoir's problematical film, *La Règle du jeu* (pluralized in English translation as *Rules of the Game*). Indeed there is an extended string of ludic performances: a fist-fight, a hunt for rabbits and pheasants (with some poaching), a round of card-games, a tangle of flirtations, and a medley of theatricals—including a masquerade, a *danse macabre*, and a Bergsonian concert from a mechanical organ. This accelerating entertainment takes place at a house-party in a chateau, where the couples keep changing partners and the servants intermingle with the guests. Renoir seems to have been inspired, by a rereading of Beaumarchais, Marivaux, and Musset, to attempt a cinematic retrieval of lost elegances and outdated amenities. But these romps are joyless, for the codes that might revive them have broken down. If the characters are at odds with one another and at loose ends with themselves, it is because no two of them seem to be playing by the same rules. Yet the party goes on and on; and when the host—a collector of music-boxes, among other things—cries, "Get this comedy stopped!," his butler—named Corneille—replies: "Which one, Monsieur le Marquis?"

It is not surprising that a storm of protest should have greeted the film's première, when it was shown on the eve of the Second World War. It is not for nothing that the phrase *jouer la comédie* has come to carry an extratheatrical meaning in French: to pull a leg, to put someone on, to act out an imposture. Renoir alerts us to reality by keeping us guessing as to where it begins and comedy leaves off. Lewis Carroll's Alice had dispelled the phantasmagoria of Wonderland or of the Looking-Glass by stopping their children's games, by telling her erstwhile playmates that they were "nothing but a pack of cards" or else, in effect, a set of chessmen. Such a reduction occurs, to some extent, whenever a curtain falls upon a last act. As the operatic clown says in *I Pagliacci*, no longer singing but speaking: "*La commedia é finita.*" There is usually a moment of vertigo, while we blink our way out of the theater. The comedy is finished; the game is over; the jig is up; and this little *commedia dell' arte* has meanwhile turned into a veristic tragedy, leaving us to infer what we have never doubted, that life is real and art is artificial.

For that very reason, art has less difficulty in living up to its self-imposed principles, arbitrary and formalistic though they must necessarily be. By momentarily playing along with them, life, which so often seems unclear and formless, can be hypothetically reshaped or—at any rate—clarified. The sense of aftermath can never last for long; it must, in due course, become a prelude to further experiences and changing moods. When Goethe first experienced the Roman Carnival, in 1787, he could hardly wait for the end to its foolishness (*Narrheit*). Having once seen it, he recorded in his Italian notebooks, he felt no interest in seeing it again. It was not worth writing about, though possibly a sketch or two of its masks and costumes might be interesting to children. Yet he was back in Rome next February to immerse himself more deeply in it, to be somewhat shaken by the spectacle, and to write an article about it which was published in 1789. He continued to harbor self-controlled reservations against this session of license (*Karnevalsfreiheit*), this resurgence of Saturnalian paganism in the holy seat of Christian observance, this temporary obliteration of polite inhibitions and social distinctions.

But the future dramatist of Faust's *Walpurgisnacht* was fascinated by the street theater of the Corso: the processions and horse races, the buffoons and dancers, the candles and confetti. Again he was relieved when Shrovetide ended; he thanked God and the church for Lent; and, looking back on the revelry that had passed "like a dream or a fairy tale," he was moved to an Ash Wednesday meditation. He visualized the long and narrow street as the allegorical scene of earthly existence. Each of us, as spectator and actor, finds his steps impeded and hemmed in by crowds of masqueraders. Our keenest pleasures are as transient as those horses racing past. Fulfilment of desire is exposure to danger; it is in moments of mad intoxication that liberty and equality can be most fully enjoyed. Goethe does not hesitate to pronounce a moral, though he does not preach a conventional morality. Faced with the fleeting, the unforeseeable, the all but unbearable carnival of life, he advises us to take advantage of the occasion, to join the masked throng while we can, to welcome this release from our unsought responsibilities, to indulge our fantasies and gratify our instincts without forgetting our human limitations.

3

THE
ARGUMENT

For any study of comedy in its historic development, Aristophanes is primordial. Not, by any means, that he is primitive, though his cloacal and homophobic snickers may seem adolescent to grown-up tastes. His Dionysiac impetus may carry us back to the very beginning of things, the brink of cosmogony. Those exposed and inflated phalli may reveal the dormant but arousable satyr in human nature. The choruses, especially when the performers are costumed as animals, can sing and dance the prehistoric wisdom of the beast fable. Aristophanes' Wasps are justly proud of the nasty stings in their tails. Yet the ritualistic formalities of his verse are elaborated to the highest degree of technical sophistication and lyrical splendor. He confesses himself a late-comer by his old-fashioned distrust of novelty, by his rearguard action against new-fangled practices and policies, plays and ideas, and by his nostalgia for the good old days of Athenian democracy and Hellenic peace.

He attained the height of satiric fantasy, literally and figuratively, in *The Birds*. Once those buoyant and harmonious creatures have built their model commonwealth in the sky, it becomes the framework for a kind of musical review, as a train of self-seeking interlopers—typical municipal offenders from Athens and elsewhere—is told off and put down. Cloud-Cuckoo-Land is strictly for the birds; utopia is not to be achieved on land or sea. For the Athenians and their successors, the play enacted a series of object-lessons in colonialism and imperialism, bureaucratic manipulation and technological exploitation. (The incomprehensible speeches of the well-meaning Triballian might even remind us of some Third World delegate to the United Nations.) The Old Comedy of Aristophanes is pointed as well as playful, not only edged with satire but reinforced with propaganda. Art is utilized by satire as a weapon, discharging pent-up animosities while attempting to score in ongoing controversies. Trying to sum it up, we feel the force of the traditional term for a synopsis of a play, *the argument*.

This means playing the game rather dangerously, and possibly deranging my suggested differentiation between the ludicrous and the ridiculous. But, as Quintilian observed, it is hard to separate laughter from derision: *"Non procul a derisu est risus."* The pleasure principle is jeopardized by apprehensions that must be surmounted or dismissed. Self-expression finds an object through aggression. Ridicule may be a sublimation of sticking pins in effigies or exhibiting public nuisances in the stocks. Aristophanic comedy moves toward a celebration, but along the way it engages in recrimination; it castigates behavior by laughing at it, with the feasting to offset the fighting. A minor poet of a later age, Jean Santeul, would solemnize this union with a Neo-Latin motto: *"Castigat mores ridendo,"* inscribed upon the curtain of a seventeenth-century theater for the leading Franco-Italian Harlequin of the day, Biancolelli known as "Dominique." Comparably, the Greek verb *kōmoidein*—"to comedize," so to speak—had been employed as a synonym for "satirize." The disparate elements in Aristophanes had come to interact dramatically, like the choruses of bathing beauties and Keystone Kops in the films of Mack Sennett.

Old Comedy was deeply rooted in archaic religion, but also in the polemical vein of iambic poetry. It left its strongest impression as a civic pillory, a vehicle for topical lampoons, and no respecter of persons in exposed positions unprotected by anything like libel laws. Gradually the personal attacks were curbed and softened into Middle Comedy, which relinquished the *parábasis*—the choric presentation of the playwright's editorial views—along with what Horace terms the "right of injury [*ius nocendi*]," and drew more upon myth and fiction, less upon current events. Seldom again would the theater, constantly subject to social pressures, address itself so boldly to personalities and politics. To be sure, Sir Robert Walpole received, from such playwrights as John Gay, the kind of taunts that Cleon had provoked from Aristophanes. Governmental reprisals thereupon brought about the Licensing Act of 1737, which established the long overlordship of the Lord Chamberlain's Office, and turned Henry Fielding away from the stage to the novel. Yet censorship could not always guard against resemblances that were more than coincidental, whereas Aesopian scrutiny could detect radical twists in the blandest story-line.

The scene might nominally be neutralized by being set in some distant country or operatic never-never-land. "As for the action . . . ," Alfred Jarry announced at the beginning of *Ubu roi*, "the place is Poland, that is to say Nowhere." Satire was described by Jonathan Swift as "a sort of *glass* wherein beholders do generally discover everybody's face but their own." That description qualifies the metaphor of the mirror by suggesting that viewers might be too self-satisfied or insensitive to feel reprimanded or offended by whatever they saw. Molière professed himself to be concerned, not with *les personnes*, but with *les moeurs*—one of those keywords which we shall be probing further. Diderot distinguished comic from tragic characters on the basis of species and individuals. This might cover the stock types of New Comedy, but it took no account of the recognizable caricatures in Old Comedy, the only comic genre that Aristotle knew when he remarked that tragic representation was nobler than life while comic was baser.

The complex structure of Old Comedy has been formulated by

F. M. Cornford with a lucid outline which has become a classic in its own right. It stimulated T. S. Eliot to his earliest dramatic endeavor, *Sweeney Agonistes: Fragment of an Agon*, and it has been theoretically extended by Northrop Frye. Its central feature, which states the issue and brings out the characters, is the *agón*, or contest. An earlier historian, Jacob Burckhardt, had emphasized what he called *das Agonale* as an institutional characteristic of ancient Greek society. Huizinga broadened this conception and applied it universally. By virtue of "the agonistic principle" the instinct for play is channeled into competitive games, most evident in organized sports but present in the more elaborate manifestations of culture. Vegetation rites were celebrated by allegorical combats between the personified seasons; fairs and rodeos and bullfights were breeding grounds for pageantry; handball games, among the Maya, terminated in the blood-sacrifice of the losing team.

Conflict is inherent in all drama, and its manner of resolution—whether it favors the protagonists or the antagonistic forces, whether we exult with the victors or condole with the losers—is another distinction between comedy and tragedy. At the core of Aristophanes' dramas it has been formalized into a great debate. The politician Cleon, scarcely disguised as "the Paphlagonian," is outeroded by the louder and cruder Sausage Seller in *The Knights*. In the more philosophical atmosphere of *The Clouds* the debaters are overt personifications of Right Reason and Wrong Reason, Dikaios Lógos and Adikos Lógos. In *The Frogs* it is a theatrical rivalry, wherein the shade of Euripides is outargued by the ghost of Aeschylus, when the poets' lines are explicitly weighed on a pair of scales. There was a Scottish parallel in the flyting, where volleys of poetic insult were formally exchanged. Individual antagonism, in a courtly milieu, would have found a structured outlet through duels, though these are more often threatened than consummated theatrically, as in *Twelfth Night*, *The Silent Woman*, and *The Rivals*. Touchstone and Mercutio spell out Shakespeare's scorn for the code of the duello, the rules of that game. Chekhov's early farce, *The Brute*, had the temerity to stage an actual duel between its hero and its heroine. Wedlock, for Punch and Judy, was an unbroken exchange of blows.

The battle of the sexes, the struggle of the classes, the clash of the generations—the leading themes of Aristophanes still frame the major problems of Bernard Shaw. The agon is the elemental plot. Now the word for plot has varying connotations in various languages: the poetic Greek *mythos*, the moralistic Latin *fabula*, the suggestive French *intrigue*, the businesslike German *Handlung*. The English monosyllable signifies originally a plot of ground, then a map or more general layout, a plan for future action, and then a nefarious conspiracy or else a mischievous design, and finally a shaping literary construction. This simplistic outline can be complicated into the "nice dilemma," the "pretty mess," or the "how-de-do" from which Gilbert extricates his Savoyards. The plot of *The Tempest* is designated by Gonzalo as a virtual labyrinth, "a maze trod indeed / Through forthrights and meanders." Similarly, Witwoud in *The Way of the World* flaunts the appropriate simile in his valedictory reaction: "I'm in a maze yet, like a dog in a dancing school." Amazement, at the dénouement, puts a finishing touch on amusement.

In *All's Well That Ends Well* the braggart soldier of fortune Parolles is much too fatalistic, when he propounds the rhetorical query: "Who cannot be crushed with a plot?" Plots can always be foiled by more ingenious counterplots. The timing of the actors' lines and business is synchronized with the thick and fast increase in the play's momentum. With the enlargement of the dramatis personae, the plotting could be doubled or multiplied still further. Traditionally, English dramaturgy has tended to foster an underplot which parodies the main plot, and which makes room for the comic episodes in Elizabethan tragedy. In the first significant example, *The Second Shepherds' Play* from Wakefield, rough-and-tumble whiles away the time until the miraculous star is sighted; the rustic dialogue, with its wintry complaints, is more redolent of Yorkshire than of the Holy Land; and the stolen sheep of the fourth and apocryphal shepherd, Mak, may be viewed in epiphanic retrospect as the secular counterpart of a more symbolic lamb.

Somewhat arbitrarily and never very conclusively, the classical five-act scheme was imposed on drama by Horatian precept. Scholiasts preferred a three-act frame: the *protasis* or exposition, the *epitasis* or complication, and the *catastrophe* or resolution. J. C. Scaliger introduced another stage preceding the final one, the *catastasis* or additional complication, thickening the plot to accommodate more characters. They would often be conversely thin; the elaboration of plot, at the expense of characterization, would ramify into the sphere of melodrama or farce. Adaptable commentators, adding the prologue to these four stages, could again reach a total of five acts. Yet the Spanish drama of the Golden Age favored a three-act partition. In the most influential of all handbooks on playwriting, *Die Technik des Dramas*, largely extrapolated from Shakespeare's craftsmanship, Gustav Freytag advocated a pyramidal scheme, which normally comprised another triad: Exposition, Climax, Dénouement. Harley Granville-Barker would agree that Shakespearean drama proceeded in three basic movements. The double plot could eke them out, but it frequently left one or two of the five acts fairly weak.

Carlo Gozzi, who specialized in transposing scenarios from the Commedia dell' Arte into literary scripts, came to the conclusion that there were no more than thirty-six dramatic situations. Goethe once discussed this proposition with Schiller, who believed offhand that there must be a greater number, but could not count up to that many after second thoughts. Can the possibilities be so limited? Not for the esthetician Etienne Souriau, who would publish a volume predicating *Les 200,000 Situations dramatiques*. Clearly, any statistical reckoning would depend upon our categories, on how far we were willing to go in abstracting or particularizing the patterns of human behavior. The comic process inevitably carries with it a considerable amount of abstraction, even as the ramification of plots is bound to have a limiting effect upon the particularity of characters. Since the agon is an argument, it must be determined in favor of one side or the other. In such a well-regulated adversary proceeding, the good guys should win out over the bad guys, according to the dramaturgic and spectatorial sympathies and antipathies.

The very simplest plot for a comedy would be a joke. We may call it a practical joke, though it usually serves no practical purpose, when some sort of hoax is acted out. Yet most of these little games, however petty, can purposefully subserve the ends of sharp practice or of conjugal hanky-panky. Such peasant pranks, narrated by jestbooks, *fabliaux*, or *Schwänke*, were pungently dramatized in the Shrovetide plays of Hans Sachs and the interludes of Cervantes. We might instance the fifteenth-century *Farce du Cuvier*, wherein a henpecked husband is constrained to draw up a list of his required household duties; when his wife falls into a washtub, he refuses to pull her out, on the legalistic grounds that such a rescue has not been nominated in the domestic contract. In spite of the title, it is not the *cuvier* but the *rollet*—not the washtub but the list—which supplies the point of the farce, the cream of the jest, the assumption of so many comedies that experience is too contingent a matter to be tabulated in advance.

The soul of the plot, in current theatrical phraseology, is the "gimmick," defined by the *Supplement to the Oxford English Dictionary* as "a tricky device." Hollywood has elevated this Bergsonian gadget to an animating idea, a veritable source of inspiration for the whole enterprise. The titular gimmick of that old Cambridge farce, *Gammer Gurton's Needle*, is the very slightest bone of contention: the misplaced article of domestic utility that turns up eventually—and feelingly—in the seat of her servingman's breeches, which Gammer Gurton has just been mending. Meanwhile the prankster, Diccon the Bedlam, whose epithet proclaims the idiocy he practices and foments, has stirred up an irrelevant hubbub among the neighboring villagers. In this case, the real antagonist is material circumstance. The role of accident places a heavy responsibility on the playwright, as we shall notice when we come to the question of chance and coincidence; but I may note in passing how much can be made of the frenzied search for the elusive and commonplace object by mentioning the chase in Eugène Labiche's *Italian Straw Hat* (*Le Chapeau de paille d'Italie*).

It takes two to make an argument, and it ordinarily takes two parties to set in motion the agonistic principle. It took no more than two actors for Aeschylean tragedy, and very little more for the Japanese Noh. Our proponent is pitted against an opponent seeking to constrict his freedom of action or to spoil his fun and games—and incidentally to impair our own innate sense of well-being, to deflect us from euphoria toward dyspepsia. That deuteragonist, given the antisocial threat he expresses and the intrusive figure he cuts, may well steal the spotlight from the protagonist. His is the stellar part in the *Dyskolos* (or *Curmudgeon*), the one complete play that has come down to us from Menander; and he is a perfect prototype for the angry old man, the *senex iratus*, of subsequent New Comedy. Lovers and merrymakers, picnicking under the pastoral aegis of Pan himself, are consistently thwarted by the malevolence of this spoilsport, Cnemon, until he chances to fall into a well—opportunely, as is pointed out. Nobody pushed him in, surprisingly enough; that was true of the housewife in the French washtub; but, on the other hand, somebody is kind enough to rescue him. The comedy is consummated by his change of heart, and the killjoy is happily exorcised by joining in the dance for a double wedding.

Shakespeare, in his most representative comedies, relies upon such tension between the lenten and the carnivalesque. In *Twelfth Night* the intruding upstart Malvolio, characterized by his name as a man of ill will, confronts the master of the Illyrian revels Sir Toby Belch, who signalizes the confrontation by exclaiming: "Care's an enemy to life." Life will go on to preserve its affirmative values by expelling the cohorts of care. A roistering exorcism will not work for Malvolio himself, though he is compelled against his nature to dress up flamboyantly and break into hideous smiles. He must face ostracism at the conclusion, with an ineffectual parting shot: "I'll be reveng'd on the whole pack of you." Life must triumph; care must become the scapegoat banished from comedy. It is a different story with the goatsong of tragedy, as it is a rebuff to the comic spirit when Falstaff is condemned to banishment. If Malvolio was, as Maria suspected, "a kind of puritan," he would have his revenge in 1642, when the playhouses were closed down by the Puritans—then, as ever, the agelastic party. But they, in turn, would suffer a putdown from the Restoration in 1660—another interval of triumph for Sir Toby's cakes and ale.

The wet-blanket cause, for Shakespeare, has an unexpected spokesman in the melancholy Jaques of *As You Like It*. Having shown a streak of misanthropy in his dialectic with Orlando the lover and with Touchstone the fool, he proposes to become a moralist and to "cleanse the foul body of the infected world / If they will patiently receive [his] medicine." This notion of a comic catharsis is borne out by the Jonsonian tropes about a satirical purge, and sealed by a notorious Elizabethan pun. Sir John Harington, poet, courtier, and inventor of the water closet, had introduced that humane contraption with a mock-heroic treatise, facetiously entitled *The Metamorphosis of Ajax*. Demythologized into plainer words, it meant the transformation of *a jakes* or privy. Hence the pun may be applied to Shakespeare's malcontent and his project in moral purgation. Not having realized this ambition, Jaques will retire from an unpurged world, step aside from the concluding capers, and—unlike Menander's Cnemon—declare himself "for other than dancing measures." If he had to dance, it would be the *pas seul* of the unpaired Bunthorne in the finale of *Patience*.

Ben Jonson addressed himself more single-mindedly than Shakespeare to the program of "comical satire," of castigation leading to correction, as set forth by his persona Asper in the Induction to *Every Man out of his Humor*. But he gradually discovered that it was easier to ridicule than to reform, and more rewarding dramatically to deal with *Every Man in his Humor*. The self-righteous asperities of his later spokesmen, such as Surly in *The Alchemist* or Wasp in *Bartholomew Fair*, do no more than demonstrate that they are out of step with most of their fellows,

nearer perhaps to the malcontents of Jacobean tragedy. His greatest grumbler, Morose in *The Silent Woman*, who can stand no
noise and is therefore almost drummed to death by crescendos of
auditory harassment, is not simply another congenital grouch.
He was the ideal "character of humor" for Congreve, just as *The
Silent Woman* was for Dryden "the pattern of a perfect play," and
his successful foil was well named Truewit, as the forerunner of
many a Restoration spark. Never was the eternal opposition of
playboy to killjoy more sharply delineated.

What these killjoys have primarily in common is that they are
agelasts. They cannot make a joke; they cannot take a joke; they
cannot see the joke; they spoil the game. Humorless and unconsciously humorous, in the Falstaffian sense of being natural butts
for wit, they cannot adapt their preconceptions to actuality, when
it unavoidably presses upon their lives. Such is Arnolphe in
Molière's *Ecole des femmes*, consummate pantaloon and jealous
guardian, making one mistake after another in his January-May
courtship of his nubile ward Agnès, who is not quite lamblike in
her docility. Ironically, her suitor Horace makes his older rival
his confidant, and talks about his progress with the young woman
step by step, but pauses because Arnolphe is so hard put to share
his mirth. "You aren't laughing enough [*Vous n'en riez pas
assez*]," says Horace to Arnolphe. How can he laugh, under the
circumstances? Since the joke is on him, he is not amused. What
is so funny about it? This is no laughing matter. But of course it is
even funnier to us, in ironic perspective, than it could be to
Horace, since we know how and why they have reached this
contretemps, and Horace does not know whom he has outrivalled.

Molière's Tartuffe would be an even more stiff-necked personage than the connubial preceptor Arnolphe, were he not—as the
subtitle warns us—an impostor, playing a double game. His
unforgettable entrance, with its opening line and ensuing business, delayed and prepared for by two acts of suspense and hear-
say, makes his hypocritical role-playing crystal-clear. Somber,
sallow, sanctimonious, with spare locks and nasal accents, he

loudly and ostentatiously orders his manservant in the wings to lock up his hair shirt and scourge; then, averting his eyes from the buxom maidservant Toinette, he offers a prurient handkerchief to cover her *décolletage*. His intrusion is more effective than Malvolio's, in dominating a household, since there is no merry crew like Sir Toby's to campaign against him—only the pert soubrette and a sardonic *raisonneur*. He is very nearly the interloper triumphant at the dispossessing climax, when he turns the tables on the householders and all but expels his erstwhile patron Orgon:

> *C'est à vous d'en sortir, vous qui parlez en maître.*
> *La maison est à moi. Je le ferai paraître.*

This pivotal couplet might be approximately rendered:

> You think you own this house. You don't any more.
> It now belongs to me; and there, sir, is the door.

It is a precarious moment: which is the scapegoat? who is excluding whom? Molière had plotted so well on Tartuffe's behalf that nothing short of royal intervention could save Orgon. Nor could the production itself have been saved from a clerical ban, if Louis XIV had not been willing to act as an offstage *deus ex machina*. Tartuffe owes his expulsion to the removal of his mask, to the pass he makes at Orgon's wife Elvire, with the admission that—like Shakespeare's Angelo, at a similar point in *Measure for Measure*—he is no angel. The comic spirit was rescued from one of its narrowest scrapes by exposing a latent streak of the playboy in the two-faced temperament of drama's most menacing killjoy.

4

BONDS OF
INTEREST

We have seen enough of the tactics deployed in the perennial war of the laughers against the non-laughers so that we might hesitate to say which takes the offensive, which the defensive side. As fellow laughers we stand committed to the playboy, viewing his eternal adversary, the killjoy, as a marplot or blocking character. Hence our hero has no choice; he too must become a plotter, if only to remove or circumvent the blocks in what might otherwise be a spontaneous, uncontested, and purely hedonistic pursuit of the pleasure principle. *Homo ludens* can protect his interests by emerging as *homo deludens*, the trickster, under the mythical patronage of Hermes or Loki. Now a trick was defined by Dr. Johnson as "a dexterous artifice." When it is not an acrobatic feat or a gainful ruse, it can be a joke, played by someone, the joker, on someone else, the joker's unwitting agonist: in tripartite Italian, *il beffa*, *il beffatore*, and *il beffato*. It is an agon, in other words, between perpetrator and victim.

The original trickster was the Devil, the ultimate villain and spinner of cosmic plots in Judeo-Christian mythology, and con-

sequently more enterprising, energetic, and colorful than its sacred figures, who were reverently treated as passive abstractions.
The Satanic adversary became one of the most popular performers in the mystery cycles, much demanded by spectators crying
out: "The Devil for my money!" His deputy, the Vice, brandish-
ing his attributive dagger of lath, was extremely active as the
principal mischief-maker in the morality plays, the half-clownish
and half-sinister agent of temptation and seduction. And since
his venue was the primrose path, rather than the everlasting
bonfire, there was little compunction in the enjoyment of his
beguiling presence. It was another of the Devil's deputies, Meph-
istopheles, who became the misguiding courier of the legendary
Faust. One of Thomas Middleton's city comedies is entitled *A
Trick to Catch the Old One*—"trick" signifying plot in both the
dramaturgic and conspiratorial senses, and "Old One" the figure
known more familiarly as "Old Nick."

Thus the challenge was raised that Mr. Punch would face in
his irascible way: to beat the Devil, to outdo Old Nick at his own
game, to escape the consequences of one's own misbehavior.
Goethe's Faust—not Marlowe's, nor most of the others—was the
casuistic exception to prove the inescapable rule. Even the most
spectacular challenger, Don Juan Tenorio, could not finally win
so diabolic a wager. However, it is significant that his originator,
Tirso de Molina, thought of him not primarily as a philanderer
or libertine, but as the arrant Trickster of Seville (*El Burlador de
Sevilla*). Glorying in the epithet, it was his favorite caprice to
trick or cheat a woman sexually (*"burlar una mujer"*). It was his
unpardonable trespass to reckon up those amorous conquests as if
they were tricks in a game of cards, and the plaints of the women
he tricked were destined to overtake him with an infernal retribution. Against a mandate of poetic justice the trickery ceases to
work, and epicurean banqueting is confounded by statuesque
morality. The obsessive sexism of Don Juan is avenged when
prostitutes refer to their clients as "tricks."

Don Juan, with the help of a tricky assistant, specialized in
sexual exploits on his own behalf. Other tricksters, more busi-

nesslike, set up as hired agents for still others, jacks-of-all-trades and johnny-do-it-alls, like Figaro the factotum in Rossini's opera. His adroit predecessor, Molière's Scapin, was himself the heir of Scappino, the professional intriguer from Naples, who fetched his name from *scappare* ("to get away"); but on the whole, *Les Fourberies de Scapin* had been modelled on Terence's play about the parasite *Phormio*. Molière's rogue, though a servant, is a free agent, officially characterized as *"valet de chambre et fourbe,"* two vocations that sort well together. He presents himself as a benevolent intermeddler who takes a friendly interest in young people: *"l'homme à m'intéresser aux affaires des jeunes gens."* Just let him handle their affairs: *"laissez-moi faire."* For he is an operator, a technician, *"un machiniste"*; he can *"machiner l'intrigue"*; and when he advises a stratagem, *"la machine est trouvée."*

This vocabulary fits in nicely with Bergson's emphasis on the mechanics of laughter. We speak too of a villain's machinations. Iago's techniques of deception may well strike us as no less comic than tragic, while the rogueries of Scapin or of the anti-heroes in picaresque fiction sometimes overstep the tenuous line between mischiefs and misdeeds. Though Ben Jonson professed to "sport with human follies," he had some difficulty in maintaining that line, especially through the dark cross-purposes of *Volpone*, which terminates all too earnestly in criminal proceedings. His more ebullient confidence-games were warranted on intellectual, if not on ethical, grounds; his gulls behave so foolishly that they sooner or later deserve to be coney-caught by his knaves. Were they not asking for it, after all? Do they not bring their comeuppance upon themselves? The hard-boiled attitude of their deceivers could be justified by a medieval Latin proverb, *"Qui vult decipi, decipiatur"*—which has been unconsciously translated into our vernacular by W. C. Fields: "Never give a sucker an even break."

Operators like to have a center, a base for their operations, even though it be denounced by one of Jonson's Puritans as a "seat of falsehood" and a "cave of cozenage." If the Alchemist's headquarters in Blackfriars (the district of London where Jonson himself resided) is a less glamorous locale than a Venetian palazzo, the self-destructing Philosophers' Stone proves to be a more tantalizing magnet than Volpone's putative will. The centripetal movement of these two neatly constructed plays relaxes in the raffish environment of *Bartholomew Fair*, where a fresh assortment of dupes gets defrauded again by a heterogeneous assemblage of sharpers on all sides. Jonson was so fond of charlatanism because he delighted in exposure, and prided himself upon knowing the knavish tricks of the illicit trades. Ethical concerns are straightened out by his last-act reversals, most of them more deftly managed than the second trial scene in *Volpone* (for which he offered excuses in his preface). But Jonson leaves us with a lingering doubt: if crooks can practice confidence-games by passing themselves off as friends and experts, ought we not to view our friends and experts with suspicion?

There is always a double satisfaction, mischievous and virtuous at once, in seeing the cheater cheated; and the irony is heightened further when the deviser is victimized by a device of his own contrivance. "For 'tis the sport to see the engineer / Hoist in his own petard." Hamlet's sentiment in dispatching Rosencrantz and Guildenstern is crudely exemplified in the primitive film of Louis Lumière, *L'Arroseur arrosé* (1895), where the amusement consists in watching a gardener get sprinkled by his own sprinkler. When Jonson transplanted his settings from Italy to England—and, in *The Alchemist*, to his own neighborhood—he explained that

> Our scene is London, 'cause we would make known
> No country's mirth is better than our own.

This declaration is not as patriotic as might superficially appear, for it continues:

> No clime breeds better matter for your whore,
> Bawd, squire, impostor, many persons more,
> Whose manners, now called humors, feed the stage.

In short, there will be much the same old cast of shady and seedy types who have been befooling one another on European stages ever since ancient times. Jonson was anglicizing them, even as Ariosto had italianized them a century before, when he set *I Suppositi* in his local Ferrara with the pictorial aid of Raphael. Their contemporary, Machiavelli, who sets his plays in a recognizable Florence, jested about such transpositions, telling the audience of *La Clizia* that Athens was now in ruins, after all—and besides, they would not understand Greek.

The Latin comedies that literature has preserved are *fabulae palliatae*, garbed in the *pallium* because they are located somewhere in Greece, commonly but not always in Athens. The more ephemeral ones, located at Rome, were *fabulae togatae*, garbed in the toga. Something of the Romans' attitude toward contemporary Greeks is revealed in the Plautine verb *pergraecari* (to revel, "to Greek it up," as it were). Solid Roman citizens looked slightly askance at such playboys, clever but slippery, cultivated but decadent; the prejudice is echoed when Shakespeare alludes to "merry Greeks." Latin prologues frequently acknowledge Hellenic sources; and Plautus in the *Menaechmi* goes out of his way to state that what must for the nonce be Epidamnus (the Adriatic port on the coast of what is now Albania) would be a different town in another play:

> *Haec urbs Epidamnus est, dum haec agitur fabula;*
> *quando alia agetur, alia fiet oppidum.*

This particular place-name will at least allow a premonitory quibble on *"damnum,"* which can be preserved if translated by "damage." Furthermore, as the prolocutor points out, any single dwelling might house a changing series of tenants. But the dwellers he mentions are the unchanged archetypes of comic tradition: *senex, adulescens, leno, parasitus.* The passage from Old to New Comedy had involved a shift from heroic and mythical to bourgeois and domestic fictions, along with the development of a standard characterization, closer links with the middle class, and increasing moments of seriousness and sentimentality.

When the ceremonious singers and dancers abandoned the orchestra, their horizontal sphere, attention had shifted to a vertical proscenium, an enlarged and ornamented stage-building, conventionally representing a busy townscape, as contrasted with the stately temple or palace of the tragic scene. From the specifications of Vitruvius to the drop curtains of music hall or vaudeville, the city street has been the main locale for comedians. Oriented by Roman convention, it led to the harbor in one direction and to the forum or marketplace in the other. For the town, more likely than not, was a seaport, whose topography bore witness to the mercantile interests of the environing culture. The doorways represented adjacent houses; it was very convenient for the lovers, in the *Miles Gloriosus*, to live next door to one another. Such domiciles would be regularly numbered by the Italians as *prima, seconda,* and *terza casa.* This arrangement promoted a good deal of neighborly byplay, many threshold-, window-, or balcony-scenes, and much ensuing curiosity as to what was going on behind the Vitruvian façades.

In the competitive arena of townsmen and tradesmen, the profit motive prevailed. When the parasite Artotragus flatters the braggart soldier Pyrgopolinices with a detailed recollection of his boasts, the boaster asks the sycophant how he happens to have such a good memory. The succinct reply is *"Offae monent* [Meals remind me]." Marx himself could not have more bluntly reduced heroics to economics. "Get money, boy," is the acquisitive attitude that Jonson inveighs against most severely through *Every Man in his Humor.* Even in the religious mysteries of the Middle Ages, the Goldsmiths' Guild was enabled to display and advertise its wares by enacting the pageant of the Magi. Another member of that trade has left his name as a byword for self-interest. In Molière's *Amour médicin,* when Sganarelle's daughter is depressed (or pretends to be for romantic reasons), he seeks the advice of his family and neighbors. M. Josse, the jeweler suggests that it would cheer the girl up if a fine necklace were purchased for her, presumably at his shop. Each of these advisers is equally venal, suggesting a remedial measure which would benefit himself or herself more than the patient. Sganarelle's reproof is a reminder that none of them speaks from disinterested concern: *"Vous êtes orfèvre, M. Josse."* You yourself are a goldsmith, you're in the business, you're the beneficiary, *cui bono?*

Oscar Wilde's definition of a cynic, as one who knows the price of everything and the value of nothing, could be interpreted as another distinction between the comic and the tragic outlook. A regard for values sounds high-minded and ennobling, while talk about prices has a reductive and deprecatory effect. When every man has his price, and every woman hers, masculine honor and feminine virtue are subject to unending devaluation. The bonds that attach human beings to one another are no stronger than the cash nexus, when the bidding goes up or the haggling goes down. This does not mean that such a realization is immoral or amoral. Rather, it stands upon high moral ground to take a low view of human nature. It consistently suspects the worst. Thus, in *L'Ecole des femmes*, when Arnolphe is jealously interrogating his silly little Agnès about her lover's advances, she confides: *"Il m'a pris le—,"* then pauses and repeats herself, still keeping the noun in suspense. After Arnolphe's suspicions have aroused the most teasing speculations as to what precisely his rival has taken in hand, it is naively revealed that the young man was clutching an innocent ribbon. Molière succeeded in scandalizing his critics by an interrupted article, that suggestive *le—*. Sterne would employ a more prurient dash to break off his *Sentimental Journey*.

The cynicism that reduces everything to sex or money ends by reducing sex to money. Not that money in itself is quite so universal; it counted for less in societies where status counted for more; but there has been no stronger incentive to selfishness, which comedy attacks in all its phases. What some of these attacks reflected was a traditional aristocratic bias against the merchant class. "If an alderman appears upon the stage," wrote

Joseph Addison, "you may be sure it is in order to be cuckolded."
His financial successes were duly paid for by his marital humilia-
tions. Money, if not the root of all evil, has been the whetstone of
wit, and the frequent source of corrupt motivation, particularly
during certain historical periods. The nineteenth-century agon of
capitalism, denounced by Marx and chronicled by Balzac, was
dramatized by such boulevard playwrights as the younger Dumas
in *La Question d'argent* and Octave Mirbeau in *Les Affaires sont
les affaires*. The monetary question is always with us, and business is proverbially business—what else? Well, it can be a pretty
name for swindling, Mirbeau tells us (*"des escroqueries qu'[on]
décore du nom des affaires"*). And the word *affairs*, which can
also denote lawsuits or love affairs, is much more resonant than
the stodgy *business*.

Pecuniary motivation may not be the final cause; but, when it
is singled out by comic low-mindedness, it helps us to see
through the verbal embellishments and the idealistic pretenses
that mask a predatory materialism. The dog-eat-dog regime of
French eighteenth-century tax-farmers, as unmasked by Lesage
in *Turcaret*, opens up a mundane vista of universal chicanery.
Frankly and exultantly the clever servant Frontin concludes to
his female accomplice: *"Nous plumons une coquette, la coquette
mange un homme d'affaires, l'homme d'affaires en pille d'autres;
cela fait un ricochet de fourberies le plus plaisant du monde."* But
how very amusing! They are fleecing a coquette, who is bam-
boozling a businessman, who is plundering innumerable others,
in the most agreeable rebound of rogueries. Truly, as the author
commented afterward, "all of the personages are vicious." This
puts them on the plane of Machiavelli's *Mandragola*, whose plot
is enmeshed in an even tighter network of mercenary motives,
though animated by an erotic impulse.

Its mainspring is the resolve of the gallant Callimaco to seduce
the virtuously named Lucrezia, money being no object and scru-
ple no obstacle. Her chastity and her husband's jealousy would
together be impregnable, were it not for her childlessness and his
frustrated philoprogenitiveness. The Machiavellian gimmick is

an equivocal nostrum, supposedly extracted from the mysterious mandrake-root, a narcotic much conjured with in fabulous lore. A potion and a poison, it is said to cure and to kill; it promises fertility in the long run, but immediate death to the woman's first bedmate after the dosage. Callimaco will play both the prescribing doctor and the connubial proxy. But how to overcome Lucrezia's stubborn honor? Others will have to join in persuading her: her own mother, her self-cuckolding husband, above all her father-confessor, Frate Timoteo. But who or what will persuade them? To Callimaco's query the plotter Ligurio offers this pithy, sharp-sighted, and all-inclusive response: *"Tu, io, i danari, la cattività nostra, la loro* [You, me, money, our wickedness, theirs]."

That complicity all but pushes the lover into the lady's bed. During their night together the Friar remains onstage before the church, noting in his anxious monologue that the statue of the Madonna has become tarnished and that her lamp has gone out. Yet, apart from those reproving symbols, everybody is happy in the end. Everyone gets what he wanted, whether in fornication, procreation, or cash. Cheerfully the unconsulted heroine accepts the situation as the will of heaven. In a modern comedy about a similar triangle, *They Knew What They Wanted* by Sidney Howard, and in its musical version, *Mos' Happy Fella*, the happiest character is the beaming foster-father of his wife's lover's child. The cynical crassness of "money talks" is wishfully mellowed by the facile sentimentalism of "love conquers all." But Machiavelli, the arch-realist of political power, in turning from *The Prince* to the bourgeoisie, was not likely to soften his own acumen. In both works he may have overstressed the trickster's wiles; yet a devil's advocate does no harm by alerting us to the ambushes of guile and venality. People do not invariably act out of self-interest, but it is safer to take that for granted than to ignore it.

As Congreve states in his preface to *The Double Dealer*, "It is the business of the comic poet to paint the follies and vices of human kind." This is no more than part of the total picture, to be sure; yet it is that part upon which worldliness thrives; and to neglect it would be to sentimentalize, to indulge in self-deception, to look upon the world with a wavering eye. In dwelling upon such matters we justify ourselves by quoting the best-known *sententia* of Terence: "*Homo sum; nihil humanum a me alienum puto.*" In the *Heauton Timorumenos* the line is spoken by an unpleasant old busybody, Chremes, as a lame excuse for his officious curiosity. The centuries seem to have redeemed it from its dramatic context and broadened it into a credo for humanists or humanitarians, so that it now expresses the fellow-feeling of anyone who is humane for anything that has to do with humanity. That includes an appalling amount of egocentricity, which runs counter to our more sociable instincts. Comedy resolves the contradiction and rights the balance by showing up our failings— and, if we consider them failings, we recognize higher standards. These are maintained, not so much by living up to them, as by shaming others who do not do so.

5

REDUCTIONS
TO FOLLY

"*La malice naturelle aux hommes est le principe de la comédie,*"
wrote the *philosophe* Marmontel, in the article on comedy that
he contributed to the rationalistic *Encyclopédie.* We need not
accept his premise, the inherent malice of human nature; but it
will aid us in understanding why the comic viewpoint had been
regarded as unworthy by philosophers ever since Plato, and why
it was so assailed by Marmontel's tender-minded contemporary,
Rousseau. Richard Steele had already campaigned for more virtuous characters, and that mode of comedy had turned out to be
not very comical. The propensity toward ridicule seems to have
been at its strongest among the satirists in the Age of Reason, and
to have been subsequently mitigated by the spreading cult of good
nature. With due regard for the more antagonistic springs of
motivation, we have been viewing them as a second principle
rather than as the first—which I take to be the pleasure principle,
as manifested in the instinct for play. Priorities are not easy to
establish, amid the tangle of motives in the dustheap of origins;

but it does seem simpler, more logical if less intellectual, to start from a spontaneous personal emotion and then proceed to adverse reactions involving others.

This is what, to my mind, puts the ludicrous a short step ahead of the ridiculous, temporarily at least. The playboy must appear and show some disposition to frolic before he can be intercepted or counterbalanced by the killjoy, though any escapade is all too likely to become an agon. Accordingly, reverting to our starting-point, we should ask ourselves what single figure precipitates the fun. We scarcely need Hazlitt to remind us of the palpable answer, "a clown," or to be reminded by Joey Grimaldi's greeting, "Hello! Here we are again!," of the clown's persistent omnipresence and the desire on the part of the audience to renew a long-standing friendship. Hazlitt suggests that we think of his stylized physique and his painted physiognomy as the features of an animated doll. As such, he would be a puppet, and ready to perform. Through his anthropological prototype, the fool, he could not have been more deeply rooted or more widely connected. The shaggy patchwork of the fool's motley garb, together with the coxcomb on his head, had preserved the attributes of a sacrificial fowl.

The original fools were harmless halfwits, who had been adopted as mascots into large feudal households. There they were petted, they kept their patrons amused, and indeed they were allowed much license for their saucy sallies. They were also thought to bring good luck and to possess unique insight. It is not without significance that the English adjective *silly* has its German cognate in *selig* (holy). For the fool was sanctified in Christ by Western tradition, and held up as a model of intellectual humility in the preaching of Saint Paul: "If anyone among you think that he is wise, let him become a fool that he may be wise." Thus his associations with wisdom have a long history—and an Attic spokesman in Socrates. As a household pet, he brought home some of those proverbial qualities which mankind shares with beasts: the stupidity of the ass and the mimicry of the ape, if not the guile of the serpent or the ferocity of the wolf. The bestiary, humanizing animals in order to moralize over them, had assigned them traits which lent themselves to comic dramatization.

Molière, who once described his own *métier* by saying that it was a strange undertaking to make good people laugh [*"c'est une étrange enterprise que de faire rire les honnêtes gens*]," significantly paralleled that description when he remarked that actors (*comédiens*) were "strange animals to direct [*étranges animaux à conduire*]." That association of ideas is worth a brief excursus. Comedy has delighted in such links between the stage and the menagerie as the theriomorphic choruses of Aristophanes. The onomatopoetic croaking of his ghostly frogs is still reechoed as a college cheer for football games at Yale: "Brekekekex, ko-ax, ko-ax." His brooding birds had progeny among dancers in *Swan Lake* and *The Firebird* and singers in *Die Zauberfläute*, with its parrot-like courtship of Papagena by Papageno. Ornithology, in modern times, has furnished descriptive totems for Chekhov's *Sea Gull*, Maeterlinck's *Oiseau bleu*, and Johann Strauss's *Fledermaus*. The *argumentum ad bestiam* has been extended into the futuristic parable of Mayakovsky's *Bedbug* and the existential absurdism of Ionesco's *Rhinocéros*.

Shakespeare, who was not above staging animal acts, arranged for Launce's dog to steal the show in *The Two Gentlemen of Verona*, and was outrivalled by Shaw in *Androcles and the Lion*. It was the more predatory characteristics that inspired the analogies in such *comédies rosses* as Henri Becque's tough comedy about ravenous types, *Les Corbeaux*. Toughness finds its emblem in the street ballad about the shark (*"Der Haifisch"*), which serves as prologue to Brecht's *Dreigroschenoper*, and it sharpens the fishy metaphor in Brecht's model, Gay's *Beggar's Opera*:

> Like pikes lank with hunger, who miss of their ends,
> They bite their companions, and prey on their friends.

The baroque skulduggery of Jonson's *Volpone, or the Fox*, is grounded in the rude beast fable of the fox and the grapes. Each of its human predators has his counterpart in the animal kingdom, as indicated by their Italian names: Voltore or the vulture,

Corbaccio or the crow, and Corvino the little raven, birds of ill omen all three, to be stung by Mosca the gadfly. On the other hand, the gentle lamb, as we have seen with the Wakefield shepherds, could become a cause of strife, despite its pastoral and paschal aspects. By confounding stolen lambs with unpaid bills, the advocate Maître Pierre Pathelin, in the fifteenth-century French farce of that name, wins the case for his client, a fraudulent shepherd—who defrauds him in turn by pursuing his courtroom advice: not to answer when questioned, simply to bleat like a sheep. (Animal voices seem to differ phonetically in different languages, so that French sheep say *"bée"* where English sheep say *"baa,"* even as English roosters crow *"cock-a-doodle-doo"*—a cry which is transposed into *"cocorico"* or *"kikeriki"* on the Continent.)

Desperately attempting to follow the thread of the argument, Pathelin's Judge has coined a catchword for withdrawing from a digression: *"Revenons à nos moutons."* Returning to the discussion, then, let us get back from the sideshow to the main tent of the circus—and, more specifically, to the clowns. Distinctions were drawn between the domesticated imbecile, who was known as "a natural," and the so-called "artificial fool," a professional entertainer who was witty in himself while pretending to be a simpleton. Shakespeare's preoccupation with fools as comic characters can be externally dated from the presence in his company of Robert Armin, a comedian who specialized in such roles. The greatest of these, King Lear's nameless Fool, is a "natural," spiritually allied to those forces of nature which blow through the tragedy, and it is his function to make the King "taste his folly." But the rest are Merry Andrews, knowing buffoons who are "wise enough to play the fool," as Viola says of Feste in *Twelfth Night*. When he accosts his mistress Olivia, who is in mourning, she is minded to dismiss him for his ill-timed levity. Whereupon he interrogates her, engaging in a bout of dialectic, and demonstrating that she is more foolish than he—foolish to mourn for a brother who, according to her own conviction, is now in heaven, and therefore better off.

It is a classical demonstration of the fool's all-purpose syllogism, repeatedly arrived at through innumerable variations, and enabling him to triumph in the last round with the retort: "*Tu quoque*. You too. You're another." You see me here with cap and bells and bauble, obviously a laughable sort of creature. But stop a minute; let us reason together; and I can show you that your thinking may not be as cogent as you think. My overt folly is but the mirror of your covert shortcomings, whatever they may be. This tactic of reduction by transference, *reductio ad stultitiam*, like the Dance of Death, embraced all the walks of society. It became a framework for ironic social surveys like the *Narrenschiff* of Sebastian Brandt, rendered into Scottish English by Alexander Barclay's *Ship of Fools*. During the Middle Ages the *Fête des Fous* had penetrated ecclesiastical sanctums. The *Enfants de Saint Souci* addressed their take-offs to political situations, and the poet Pierre Gringore did not hesitate to depict the King as *Le Prince des Sots*, the Pope as *La Mère Sottie*, and the populace as *La Sotte Commune*—all fools, all reveling in their foolishness. If you had occasion to feel foolish, you could feel that you were in good company. Folly was looked upon as an amiable and ubiquitous weakness. Twentieth-century theatrical producers could point back a long distance when they advertised their entertainments as *Follies*.

The enigmatic locution *ducdame* is explained by Shakespeare's Jaques as a charm for summoning fools into a circle. From the learned increment of further explanation by Shakespearean scholars, we may infer that it has achieved its purpose. The antics of the Marx Brothers (and antic meant a grotesque display) were most commonly heralded by a title which promised little else except utter nonsense, conveyed through a variety of scatterbrained metaphors: *The Coconuts, Animal Crackers, Horse Feathers, Monkey Business, Duck Soup*. A familiar paradox is expounded in Sir David Lyndsay's *Satire of the Three Estates*: "*Sapientia hujus mundi stultitia est.*" The wisdom of this world is indeed mere stupidity in the otherworldly light of Christian ethics, as expounded by Saint Paul. Consequently, in the dialogue of John Heywood, *Witty and Witless*, it is the latter who asserts the decisive *tu quoque*, and who esteems the court jester Will Summers above King Solomon in all his sagacity: "Bet be sot Summers than sage Solomon."

This doctrine was combined with the Socratic posture, the self-deprecating avowal of ignorance as a precondition of true knowledge, to produce that ambiguous masterpiece of Renaissance humanism, Erasmus' *Laus Stultitiae*, or *The Praise of Folly*. Whether it actually glorified folly or else devalued wisdom, it conceived the world *sub specie comoediae* as a series of histrionic performances in which everyone had been cast: "And what is all this life but a kind of comedy wherein all men walk up and down in one another's disguise and act out their respective parts till the property-man brings them back to the tiring-house?" Erasmus was reviving the Greek conception of irony exemplified by the *eíron*, the dissembler who knows more than he slyly admits, in polar contradistinction to the *alazón*, who bombastically claims more than he can fulfil. The one takes a self-protective stance; the other goes on a rampage; and it is the agon between them that turns the ironist into a satirist and turns the impostor into an object of satire, Aristophanic or otherwise. Hence, as even Don Quixote realized, "the most artful part in the play is that of the fool."

Yet in essence—or, more corporeally, at bottom—the clown is a butt; by the brusque definition of Saint John Chrysostom, the most eloquent denouncer of drama among the Church Fathers, it is "he who gets slapped." This implies a knockabout relationship with someone else wielding the slapstick, that venerable wand of lath which produces so resounding a smack. When left to himself, and not pushed around by the others, he is likely to become his own victim, like the once-famous Grock as the would-be pianist whose worst enemy is his piano. But whenever the clown is a soloist, he becomes all the more involved with his audience—more mobile, if less voluble, than the latter-day stand-up comedian. Bergson's first exercise in laughter is illustrated by the jack-in-the-box, who does nothing but pop up; then someone must put him down in order that he may pop up again. Bergson's second exercise is modelled on the jumping jack, where attention shifts to the agent who pulls the strings, the one who turns the trick: from the passive to the active role, the tricked to the trickster, the gull to the coney-catcher.

Comedy-teams are not necessarily conjoined in mutual antagonism or conflict of interest. Presently we shall be considering masters and servants, who hunt in couples, and lovers and sweethearts, who incline to duets, clinches, and *pas de deux*. However, a comic speaker needs a straight man (or woman) to feed him or her the lines, for whom it is not always easy to keep a straight face. (We do our best to avoid sexism, but all too inadequately, because our subject is full of it.) He or she is often tempted to mug or grimace—to "catch flies," as they say when an actor upstages his fellow actors by improvising a bit of business. The stooge becomes a comic in his own right. Ostensibly, the pudgy Oliver Hardy might seem much funnier than the insipid Stan Laurel; but the double-takes and slow burns end by reinforcing the deadpan partner's fumbling ineptitudes; and it is known that Laurel was really the brains of that act. The story is told of the playwright Georges Feydeau that the actor Sacha Guitry once asked him for a dramatic vehicle. "Very well," Feydeau replied. "But you understand that a farce has two main roles, the person who gets kicked on the backside and the person who administers those kicks. It is the former who gets the laughs." And Guitry is reported to have dropped his request.

The traditional clever servant, the luckless heir to Greek and Roman slaves, was continually threatened with physical chastisement, with the whip if not the mill. He could enjoy his revenge through Molière's notorious *truc*, where the curmudgeon Géronte is tied up in a bag and soundly beaten by the rogue Scapin. But Scapin must repent and undergo a mock-death to attain forgiveness and reconciliation. Mr. Punch can beat his wife, their baby, the very devil, and get away with it. Consequences are suspended—for a while, anyway—and there is a general sense of liberation when he announces Satan's death:

"We can now all do as we like." Now it is the top dog, again the underdog, who earns our sympathy and is rewarded by our laughter. The partnership of *Waiting for Godot,* in the absence of the awaited third party, is more or less equally matched, even to their reduplicating nicknames, Didi and Gogo. Vladimir and Estragon are a pair of preconditioned losers, like the thieves that flanked the crucifixion; but it is Gogo who elicits the last weary laugh by an anticlimactic effort to hang himself with the rope that has, up to this critical moment, been holding up his trousers.

The most exemplary of modern comedians, Charlie Chaplin, managed to incorporate an agon—nay, virtually a class-struggle—within his fragile, shabby-genteel figure: the threadbare little tramp with the minute moustache and the mincing manners, crowned by a bowler hat and armed with a walking-stick, politely smiling, fastidiously tipping his hat, and waddling away into the sunset. Let us not forget that he began his picaresque career as a heavy English swell, a drunken music-hall toff. This dualism would be grandly externalized in *The Great Dictator,* wherein he plays the dual role of the *eíron,* the little Jewish barber, and the *alazón,* Hynkel/Hitler. To cite some early titles, the contrast he sustained was between *The Tramp* or *A Dog's Life,* on the one hand, and *Easy Street* or *The Idle Class* on the other—in short, between rags and riches. He embodied survival, if not triumph, for life's waifs and strays, for all the fall guys, sad sacks, and lame ducks who ever tried to dodge a cop. If the hobo is the poor man's playboy, his killjoy is the policeman. Inadvertently, by picking up a red safety flag which has fallen from a passing truck, Charlie finds himself leading a march of radical protest in *Modern Times.* *City Lights* concludes with a wistful recognition scene; the heroine is, as usual, a female waif; and here a pathetic derelict, the Blind Girl, recovers her sight and suddenly realizes that her gallant benefactor, her good angel, her Prince Charming is— well, nobody but Charlie Chaplin, who can only smile and tip his hat and walk away.

With simple clowns—say, with Sancho Panza in his naive beginnings,—the unavoidable discomfiture was less absurd than it would become for so pretentious a master as Don Quixote. Pretentiousness is a way of boasting, a form of affectation, which in its turn—so Fielding affirmed—is a source of "the true ridiculous." Molière elaborates on it in the fopperies of his *petits marquis* or the precious tastes of his bluestockings, exposing them to bourgeois common sense in *Les Précieuses ridicules* and *Les Femmes savantes*. In *Le Bourgeois gentilhomme*, where the situation is reversed, the Music Master, the Dancing Master, and the Fencing Master, all of them hired to polish their middle-class pupil in the courtly graces, get into an ungentlemanly wrangle with regard to their respective fields of accomplishment. They appeal to the considered judgment of a new mentor, the Master of Philosophy, who responds by asserting his own preeminence with such unphilosophical fury that nothing can be heard above the belaboring commotion except their ineffectual cries of mollifying entreaty: "*M. le Philosophe! M. le Philosophe! M. le Philosophe!*" If his affectations of wisdom are reducible to another folly, so much for the consolations of philosophy!

The inflated claims of competing *métiers* invite the kind of exposure to which Ben Jonson builds up through the intimidating jargon of *The Alchemist*. But any vocation can be exposed as a racket, when it overstates its own importance. W. S. Gilbert subjected the leading professions to self-exposure—"The army, the navy, the church, and the stage"—through the confessional patter-songs of his avuncular light baritone in the parts created by George Grossmith: the First Lord of the Admiralty, the Lord Chancellor, the Lord High Executioner, not to mention "the model of a modern major general." True to Gilbert's antipodal outlook, the only romantic hero to emerge from the Savoy Operas was the heartbroken jester Jack Point in *The Yeomen of the Guard*. As a briefless barrister, Gilbert poked fun at the law; as a prudent and rather prudish Victorian, he shied away from the church, substituting esthetes for rival curates in dramatizing *Patience* from one of his *Bab Ballads*. To portray the artist as conniving, like Bunthorne, in a self-confessed "esthetic sham" was a coy admission of British philistinism; and when Gilbert adverted to pirates and gondoliers, familiar satire dissolved into exotic whimsy.

Medicine is the profession that held a special fascination for those who dared to confront it, for no one more than for Molière. The indispensable clyster, or enema, is as frequent a property in his comedies as the phallus had been in those of Aristophanes. Doctors were the descendants of shamans, closely associated with powers of life and death, whose mysterious pretensions were undercut by their manifest quackery. Apothecaries were descended from the *ciarlatani*, those charlatanical vendors of nostrums who combined showmanship with salesmanship, so volubly mimicked by the medicine-show in Jonson's *Volpone* or Molière's *Amour médecin*. What the latter scorned and derided in his medical men was their distrust of empirical experience and their dependence on antiquated authority. The myopic bookishness of their diagnostic methods, which started from—and never departed from—Hippocrates ("*Hippocrate dit . . .*"), is shown up by the pragmatic flexibility of Sganarelle, when forced to pose as a physician in *Le Médecin malgré lui.* Having mistakenly located the heart on the wrong side of the body (i.e., the right side), he brazenly covers up his mistake by claiming to be in the vanguard of scientific progress, which has changed all that ("*nous avons changé tout celà*").

Those who believe that physicians have succeeded in freeing themselves from the moulds of professional deformation or the trade secrets of a closed corporation should look again at Shaw's discussion of contradictory diagnoses and prognoses, prescriptions and therapies, in *The Doctor's Dilemma.* His doctors, true to his Olympian vantage-point, are neither unsympathetic nor un-self-critical. "We're not a real profession," Sir Colenso Ridgeon admits, "we're a conspiracy." Their professionalism, for better and worse, is pitted against the bohemianism of Shaw's self-romanticized artist, Louis Dubedat, and the result is a characteristic stalemate. Molière has been updated but hardly refuted by Jules Romains, himself a medico by training, in *Knock, ou la Triomphe de la médecine.* When its malpractitioner glibly boasts about his rural clinic that "all the rules of modern hygiene are observed," he is reaffirming the comic distance between the literal regulations and the experimental facts. Modes of treatment may vary, but not the location of the heart.

The endeavor to learn or teach life's lessons gets caught up at times in the mindless rote of hypothetical schemes or automatic systems, which encourage it to overlook the matter-of-fact and down-to-earth pragmatism of common sense. The quest for knowledge all too readily freezes into an *idée fixe*, which needs to be unfixed, unfrozen, or liberated. Hence schools can be the incubators of pedantry, and the pedant is the silliest of fools—the very opposite of Socrates—because he pretends to be truly wise, though such knowledge as he possesses is of the most narrowly specialized kind. There is an earthy satisfaction in out-smarting the smart-aleck, as with the peasants' son, so vain about his university degree, who returns to his rustic village for a comedown in Ludvig Holberg's *Erasmus Montanus*. The fiasco of the crotchety schoolmaster Holofernes accentuates the paradoxical moral of *Love's Labor's Lost*: that feminine companionship is really more instructive than academic retreat. Molière's *Ecole des femmes* and *Ecole des maris*, like "the scandalous college" in Sheridan's *School for Scandal*, use the pedagogical concept as a background for studies in manners.

The stage could thus present, like the *Bildungsroman*, the disillusioning record of an educational pursuit, which finds a more meaningful discipline in the school of experience. Rousseau controverted such a presumption when he called the theater *"une école de vices et de mauvaises moeurs,"* stubbornly confusing the depiction of misconduct with its perpetration. Eugène Ionesco has done his best and worst to live up to this indictment in the mad curriculum of *La Leçon*, even more intimidating in French than in English: *"L'arithmetique mène à la philologie, et la philologie mène au crime."* Again the example had been set by Aristophanes. *The Clouds* had reduced a school of thought, the philosophy of the Sophists, to the burlesque of an academy, the Phrontistérion or think-tank of the pseudo-Socrates. Old Comedy, so heavily institutionalized in its format, centered its issues on local institutions or community enterprises, such as the sexual strike of the women against the war in *Lysistrata*. These large-scale reductions to folly could deal with the theater, as in the repeated critique of Euripides, but scarcely with acting, which had yet to acquire the status of a profession.

6

THE TRUTH
OF MASKS

We think of acting as impersonation, and then we begin to wonder whether such an aim can better be achieved by a process of emotional identification, as Stanislavsky advises, or by the discipline of artistic technique, as Diderot has argued. There must be a certain inner tension whenever anyone tries to convince others that he or she is really—for a stated interval—someone else. And there may remain some gap in that attempt, some degree of disparity between the person who does the acting and the personage that he or she enacts. This would be perceived as an imperfection in serious drama, which requires implicit acceptance for its psychic involvements. In comedy there is plenty of room for the actor to revert to himself or else to exaggerate his portrayal, to step out of his part or to overdo it. He can be disengaged from dramatic contexts much more easily than the tragic protagonist. And, whereas the latter is generally expected to display a prepossessing appearance, the comedian seems to thrive upon queer looks and even physical deformities, like Punchinello's hooked nose and hunched back.

The early actor—originally an amateur—derived his personality from his mask, even as our word itself derives from *persona*, the Latin noun for mask, stemming from the verb *personare* ("to sound through"), which recalled its amplifying function in outdoor performance, through emblematic lips turned downward for tragedy and upward for comedy. Wilde has stressed, in this connection, the paradox of disguises conveying truths. For Old Comedy the masks could be quite specific, whether they depicted actual people or transformed the choric celebrants. In New Comedy they represented social types. There were exactly forty-four of these, according to the rhetorician Pollux; and the distribution was an interesting reflection of the dramatis personae, if not of society at large: ten old men, ten young men, three old women, fourteen young women, and seven slaves. Each of them was costumed in an appropriate color, depending on age, sex, and status. That is not an extensive but rather a limited number, if we assume that drama should present in some fullness the permutations and the interactions of human behavior. It committed dramatists to the assumption that human nature changed little from one epoch to the next.

This sentiment was voiced and handed on by a distich from Ovid's *Amores*, translated by Christopher Marlowe and slightly revised by Ben Jonson:

Whilst slaves be false, fathers hard, and bawds be whorish,
Whilst harlots flatter, shall Menander flourish.

But that does not rule out the possibility of Menander becoming outdated by future changes of heart or of moral climate—nor the blank fact, for whatever you want to make of it, that most of his work has been lost. Terence, through his actor-spokesman in *Heauton Timorumenos*, confessed his boredom with such stereotypes. Nonetheless he depended upon them and frequently ticked them off in his prologues, as did Plautus, and as neoclassical playwrights would still be doing when New Comedy had become the oldest of living dramatic traditions: *senex, adulescens, servus, parasitus, matrona, virgo, ancilla, meretrix, et caetera.* Ben Jonson, pledged to the presentation of *Every Man in his Humor*, theorized on how temperament could be determined by physique, and kept a connoisseur's eye out for *tics*, compulsions, idiosyncrasies, and monomanias. Bertolt Brecht would bear witness that some of these behavioral constants were still operative during the twentieth century, when the opening stage direction of *Die Dreigroschenoper* called for beggars to be begging, thieves stealing, whores whoring, and everyone doing his or her thing (*"Die Bettler betteln, die Diebe stehlen, die Huren huren . . ."*).

When Sidney defended poetry, his characterology was directly drawn from the Terentian repertory: "a niggardly *Demea*, . . . a crafty *Davus*, . . . a flattering *Gnatho*, . . . a vainglorious *Thraso*"—prime examples of the miser, the clever servant, the parasite, and the braggart captain. Terence's Elizabethan translator, Richard Bernard, would moralize the spectacle, justifying their dramatized misbehavior as a series of didactic case-histories for readers and spectators: "He will tell you the nature of the fraudulent flatterer, the grim and greedy old sire, the roistering ruffian, the mincing minion, and the beastly bawd, that in telling the truth by these figments men might become wise to avoid such vices and learn to practise virtue." These testimonials, in their very eagerness to ward off the puritanical opposition, strike a note of apology, probably overstating the moralistic intentions and overrating the melioristic effects. We have agreed that comedy butters no parsnips, and have entertained some reservations with regard to its authors' claims as reformers.

But decorum, the observance of the proprieties, is a set of dramaturgic as well as ethical norms, presupposing that everybody should speak and behave—and, if it is a comedy, should stay—in character. If it is a tragedy, he or she may change and grow and develop, in accordance with the temporal span. Comic characterization seems to be more spatially oriented, by contrast, more static and two-dimensional. If there is any alteration, it is brought about through metamorphosis rather than growth: through sudden conversion or unmasked disguise or magical enchantment, like Bottom's translation into—what he has innately been all along—an ass. George Whetstone, advising other playwrights in the dedication to his *Promos and Cassandra*, takes an almost behavioristic stance: "To work a comedy kindly, grave old men should instruct, young men should show the imperfections of youth, strumpets should be lascivious, boys unhappy, and clowns should speak disorderly, intermingling all these actions in such sort as the grave matter may instruct and the pleasant delight."

It may be more than a coincidence that, whenever the "character"—the generalized prose portrait—has flourished as a literary genre, it has been closely allied with comedy. We could make some pertinent cross-references from Menander to Theophrastus, from Molière to La Bruyère, or from Ben Jonson to Sir Thomas Overbury. In the two modern instances, the analytic prose seems to come shortly after the dramatic representation. In the formative case of Menander, he had learned from Theophrastus, who had been Aristotle's disciple in his day, and had sketched his psychological portraits to exemplify his teacher's ethics. Browsing through those thirty *Characters*, beginning with the Dissembler or *eíron*, we may notice how readily their lineaments could be brought to life on the stage. The Miser, the Flatterer, the Rustic, how familiar they already seem! As for the Blusterer or *alazón*, forever showing off and dropping names, ranting about his exaggerated campaigns and fictitious investments, pretending he wants to sell his rented house because it is too small for his needs, there he stands, a histrionic persona, larger and finally more single-minded than life.

Typologies will vary in different climes and times. We are told that the Peking Opera, possibly the most conventionalized of living theaters, depends upon four main actors: the *sheng* (male lead), the *dan* (female lead traditionally acted by a male, notably Mei Lan Fang), the *jing* (heavy, literally "painted face"), and the *chou* (clown). Anglo-American stock companies trouped along for generations with casts that had been comparably standardized: the Leading Man and Lady, the Juvenile, the Ingenue, the

Heavy, the Low Comedian, the Soubrette, the First and Second Walking Gentlemen, seasoned troupers all. They would probably have had little difficulty in casting a forgotten play from the age of Queen Anne by one William Taverner. Its very title evokes a reappearing pattern, *The Maid and the Mistress*, while its prologue undertakes to show us persons who are—*mutatis mutandis*—durable if not immutable. Though the descriptive vocabulary has dated, we should not find them too difficult to recognize today:

> The Fop, the Rake, the Country Squire and Cit,
> The Real Blockhead and Conceited Wit,
> The Jilting Mistress and the Faithless Wife
> Shall see themselves all painted to the life.

Bergson has pointed out how many comedies have been, or could be, characterized by generic epithets, such as *The Miser* or *The Liar* (there are plays under the latter heading by Lope de Vega, Corneille, and Goldoni). *The Impostor*, one might add, would cover a multitude, since deception by means of personification is so frequent a resort.

Crossing back to the other side of the footlights, we might observe that the Savoy Operas, though they range considerably in their themes and settings, had to reincarnate in each production the existing personnel of the D'Oyly Carte Company. There was always the skipping and tongue-wagging Grossmith part, always the stout contralto singing Ruth, Katisha, Lady Jane, Little Buttercup, and the Fairy Queen, and further parts to suit the other singers. When Hamlet welcomes the Players to Elsinore, he gives us a glimpse of how a script might be adapted to a band of strollers—the King, the Lady, the Fool, the Humorous Man— and the monologue of Shakespeare's humorous Jaques envisages the seven ages of man as predictable scenes in the *theatrum mundi*. One company could scarcely carry out an adequate repertory, unless it was constituted to meet such demands of typecasting. On the other hand a playwright, working with a given group of players, could tailor his playwriting to fit their talents. I have suggested how the acting specialty of Robert Armin might have contributed to the creation of Shakespeare's fools. In Molière's *Fourberies de Scapin*, when Zerbinette unwittingly and gleefully reveals the big joke to its victim, her *"crise de fou rire"* was written in for an actress, Mademoiselle Beauval, who specialized in peals of coloratura laughter.

Actors and actresses came into their professional existence without benefit of scripts: ancient mimes and rope-dancers, medieval *jongleurs* and mountebanks, who mingled patter with their gymnastic routines. Under a much later dispensation, W. C. Fields would be trained as a juggler and Buster Keaton as an acrobat. Like Charlie Chaplin, like the original fools, they retained their personal identities, regardless of their elaborating milieux; they remained themselves, though their theatrical selves were caricatures of ordinary humanity—and caricature is a kind of Aristotelian mean between the laughable and the ugly. Comics preserve their individuality through distinctive mannerisms, vocal eccentricities, whimsical dress, odd make-up, over-emphatic gestures, and idiosyncratic bodily traits. Yet there cannot be genuine drama until they are drawn together in their collective folly, until the entertainers pool their skills by forming troupes. A transitional role was enacted by Angelo Beolco, whose stage-name, *Il Ruzzante*, could be a synonym for "the Playboy." It was he who blended his peasant monologues in the Paduan dialect with the literary comedy (*commedia erudita*), which Italian men of letters were reviving at sixteenth-century courts. And Italy, for historical and cultural reasons, has been central to the continuities of occidental drama.

There the richest and ripest development was the popular Commedia dell' Arte, *arte* standing first and foremost for theatrical professionalism. This was, above all else, the comedians' comedy, an actors' and actresses' theater. Though it revivified the prototypes of New Comedy, it had renewed their strength by touching the soil, in the qualified sense that it had evolved when the local performers teamed up together while preserving the dialects and characteristics associated with their several regions. Ethnic disparities have never ceased to lend themselves to humorous exploitation; closer to home the scene would be variegated by the emergence of blackface minstrels and a succession of American immigrants from many other lands. Even within the boundaries of seventeenth-century Italy, as Carlo Goldoni noted in autobiographical retrospect, one of the two *vecchi* came from the financial capital Venice, the purse-proud but suggestible Pantalone, while the other heavy father (or hoodwinked husband) came from Bologna, seat of a famous law school, the pettifogging and bumbling Doctor Graziano. Naturally, there were many conniving attendants or *zanni*, but Goldoni scaled them down to two abiding types: the wily Brighella and the naive Arlecchino, both of them from the mountain town of Bergamo—one of those conventionally funny habitats, like Gotham or Dubuque.

Each member of that quartet bears his peculiar marks of identification: the baggy breeches that came to be known as pantaloons, the wine stain on Graziano's bulbous nose, Brighella's dapper livery, and Arlecchino's lozenge-patterned attire. All four wore vizards over their unmistakable faces, in contradistinction to the unmasked visages of the straight characters, preeminently the Inamorata and the Inamorato. Casts included a good many other colorful figures, but Goldoni clarifies the action by concentrating upon the relationship between *vecchi* and *zanni*, and this proves to be a reenactment of the perennial agon between a rigid *alazón* and a flexible *eíron*. The elders are householders, pillars of the establishment, ever ready to thwart their juniors, the wayward lovers, the natural pleasure-seekers. But the seniors foil themselves by departing from their sphere and seeking youthful—normally sexual—pleasures, prodded and cajoled by their hustling retainers, the mischievous go-betweens. Hence the mischief-maker takes over the central role, ultimately magnified out of all proportion. Busybodies of all sorts follow the footsteps of Arlecchino and Brighella, some of whom are dynamic enough to achieve independent standing, like Scaramuccia and Pulcinella.

The most important innovation of the Commedia dell' Arte, overcoming a long and stubborn taboo, was its introduction of the actress. When convention, social and theatrical, assigned the feminine roles to men or boys, the effect must have been highly stylized if not simply awkward, or else self-consciously comical. Not only was it more natural and graceful to cast women as women, but it must have had a liberating impact. The Prima Donna won fame and admiration in the dazzling person of Isabella Andreini, whose husband Francesco led the most prominent troupe, the Gelosi ("anxious to please"), and who himself appeared in the swashbuckling guise of Capitano Spavento della Vall' Inferno (Captain Fright of Hell's Valley). Ten or twelve of these performers were recruited to make up a company, each of them enacting his or her established persona throughout a varied and abundant repertory. The notion of living the part takes on a special significance, with actors who invariably maintained a fixed identity, while reacting to a continuous sequence of changing plights. Our consciousness of human limitations is reinforced when, whatever the story, the selfsame cast reappears. Generalizations attest how small the world is; questions then arise as to who or what might have been left out.

If the stage truly represents a world, it should theoretically contain at least a representative sampling of everyone and everything. But individualism is reduced by being typed, even as the Aristophanic Socrates was shrunken into a Sophist. The improvisation of the Commedia dell' Arte, like that of good jazz musicians, could not have been sustained without the utmost in individual skill—that was the *arte*—plus the sort of timing that comes through seasoned experience in working intimately with the same ensemble. The *scenario*, an outline of the plot that was posted in the wings, was filled in with the help of *concetti*, flowery passages memorized by the lovers, and *lazzi*, standard gags perpetrated by the buffoons. Here, if anywhere, comedy was resolved into its unitary components. But performances were not confined to comedy as such. The major collection of *scenari* edited by Flamineo Scala was announced on its title page with a traditional subdivision into comical, pastoral, and tragical amusement (*"la ricreazione comica, boscoreccia, e tragica"*). How far these could stray from bourgeois precincts to realms of fantasy would be shown by the fairy-tale dramas or *fiabe* of Count Gozzi, which have chiefly survived in the form of libretti for two well-known operas, Puccini's *Turandot* and Prokofiev's *Love of Three Oranges.*

One of the most influential links in theatrical genealogy was the apprenticeship of the young Molière to Tiberio Fiorilli, the starring Scaramuccia of the Comédiens Italiens at Paris, who in his eighties could still perform the *lazzo* of slapping his face with his foot. Linkage with the Italians could be traced through the rising fortunes of Pedrolino, originally a minor Neapolitan clown, who was gallicized, refined, and blanched into the wistful Pierrot, to be all but apotheosized in the paintings of Watteau. His enactment in the Théâtre des Funambules, by the nineteenth-century mime Deburau, would be replicated by Jean-Louis Barrault, as dramatized by Jacques Prévert and filmed by Marcel Carné in *Les Enfants du Paradis.* Pierrot's fellow valet, Arlecchino the Bergamask, has travelled even farther; not unlike Punch, the quondam Pulcinello of Naples, he became a naturalized Englishman through John Rich's spectacular pantomimes, and—with the *servetta* Colombina/Columbine as his partner—danced his way through hundreds of harlequinades. It became a national custom in England for families to celebrate the day after Christmas (Boxing Day) by attending the entertainments at which Harlequin presided. In Germany he was less conspicuous; but, through a controversy among the critics, and largely through a printed monologue by Justus Möser, he became an apologist for caricature in art and for the esthetics of the grotesque.

All of these maskers contributed, each in his own way, to the sweeping demonstration of Erasmus that "the greatest part of mankind are fools." Having immersed ourselves for a while in their follies, as well as in the concomitant rogueries, it might make a modicum of sense to put in a word of recapitulation at this mid-point. Starting from the pure, the natural fool, indulging in artless play, our next stage was that of the artificial fool, engaged in artful play. He became the clown, and his art became comedy, bringing others—more pretentiously—into that charmed circle, reducing their pretensions to folly, and thereby effecting a transference from the domain of the ludicrous to that of the ridiculous. Insofar as the macrocosm of society gets reflected in the microcosm of drama, the dramatis personae represent a selection if not a cross-section, a reduction to types and even—at their most typical—masks, satirizing professional deformation and institutional abuse. But the theater itself is an institution with a long and multiform history of practice, from which I have been culling examples, not to elucidate plays or evaluate playwrights but to sketch a theory of sorts—or, at any rate, a paradigm compounded of many simples. My theoretical concern has therefore been to isolate and illustrate a few first principles and basic elements. For the rest, I shall be concerned with how they interact in comic structures of varying modality and increasing complexity.

7

DUPLICITIES

What's in a name? A great deal, as no one knew better than that writer who bore so odd a surname as Shakespeare. Not only have his characters' names become household words, but some of them have become bywords for persons who share their characteristics: a toper is a Falstaff, an extortioner a Shylock, a married man a Benedick (the last, commonly twisted into Benedict, an *a fortiori* case, noteworthy for giving up a declared resistance to matrimony in *Much Ado about Nothing*). In much the same way, comic characters have come to serve as godfathers for satirical journals: *Punch, Figaro, Simplicissimus*. How they were named in the first place is an aspect of the writer's craft which has a decorum of its own. It is not so simple as Wilde's dandies believed, when they expected automatic reform just as soon as they were rechristened Ernest. Could Jack and Algy ever have lived up to the baptismal expectations of Gwendolyn and Cecily? It was at once an advantage and a disadvantage for the permanent casts of the Commedia dell' Arte to be recognized in advance by their stage-names. Charles Lamb, a much better dramatic critic than a dramatist, wrote an unactable drama, *Mr. H—*, in which the protagonist's tragic fate is to have a comic name.

Donatus, the grammarian of New Comedy, prescribes that "names should fit." Terence's slaves bear servile designations, often indicating their foreign origins: thus Geta from the Goths. "*Davus sum, non Oedipus*," the slave announces in the *Andria*, implying furthermore that it will be a comedy, not a tragedy. Hence the subject-matter can be fictitious, and the nomenclature is not handed down but made—as it were—to order. Aristotle had indeed allowed that comedies might use invented names. Erotium seems to be an appropriate choice for a prostitute of Plautus; Chremes, for some tedious elders in Terence, both denotes and echoes a clearing of the throat. With a similar type Molière simply adapted the Greek for "old man" into the French Géronte; T. S. Eliot has poetized a dwarfish descendant as "Gerontion." Molière's ultimate medico bears the cathartic cognomen, Dr. Purgon; his miser, Harpagon, is so denominated after the unusual Plautine verb *harpago* (to plunder); and his would-be country gentleman, Monsieur de Pourceaugnac, encloses a porcine root between an aristocratic particle and a regional suffix. Aristophanes, whose dramaturgy has been compared with political cartooning, fitly labelled his man of the people Demos. For his feminist and pacifist leader he coined an epithet, Lysistrata, disbander of armies.

Comedy has habitually set great store by onomastics, the science of naming, and by what the Germans call speaking names, *redenden Namen*. In English we may call them charactonyms, names that describe the characters. These were downright homiletic labels in the moralities, becoming more sophisticated with Jonsonian usage, which was carried on through the Restoration into the eighteenth century. Knightly titles provided a twofold opportunity, from Sir Politick Wouldbe through Sir Fopling Flutter to Sir Mulberry Hawk. Not all comic appellations were pejorative; the brilliant couple in *The Way of the World* is romanticized; Millamant suggests a thousand lovers, Mirabel the admiration of the belles. On the less romantic side of Congreve's cast, Lady Wishfort invites a reduction to words of one syllable: "wish for it." What she wishes for, and that she wishes vainly, are equally clear. In John Gay's underworld the sharks and pikes are baptised with a more than Dickensian aptness: the informer Peachum, the jailer Lockit, the pickpocket Filch, the street-walker Trapes. With a difference, in Sheridan's *School for Scandal*, both of the brothers—the sincere Charles and the hypocritical Joseph—uphold their family name Surface, so suitable to a comedy of manners. Few who evoke the spirit of Lady Bountiful actually recall her appearance in Farquhar's *Beaux' Stratagem*.

Bernard Shaw was never averse to exploiting the tricks of his trade. His denominations are less explicit but often forceful: Brassbound, Undershaft, Shotover, and—quite expressly, for a surgeon—Mr. Cutler Walpole. Gogol, who delighted in verbal devices of this kind, went so far as to name a pack of cards in *The Gamblers*, adding the Russian patronymic: Adelaida Ivanovna. This was to take a game quite seriously, as we do when we go to the theater, which may ask us to believe for a while that a piece of cardboard is a human countenance. We may balk at accepting conventions—as if we could live without them, as if our lives were not structured by them! "Then are all things represented by counterfeit," wrote Erasmus in *The Praise of Folly*, "yet without them there would be no living." But this is to look upon life itself as a series of disguises. There is a sense in which comedy may be said to dehumanize whatever it touches. Its masks seem more like caricatures than characters, its stylization of experience seems to be an abstraction from it. But the only choice we have, George Santayana observed, is "between the mask and the fig leaf," between assuming identity or covering nakedness, and the fig leaf is only "a more ignominious mask."

Pirandello must have been thinking in such terms when he styled his plays "naked masks [*maschere nude*]"—as who should say that the final reality eludes us, that we are lucky if we are left with a painted approximation. Taken at its face value, a mask is a *persona*, the image of a personality. Reconsidered in denuding depth, it is an impersonation, and therefore a means of deception. Such deceits have never troubled classicists, who have always accepted that element of the fictitious in fiction, or of make-believe in poetry, which disgruntled Rousseau and led him to denounce actors as deceivers. Of course they enacted deceptions over and over again. The valet Mascarille—note his name—masquerades as a nobleman to expose the pretensions of Molière's *Précieuses ridicules*. Congreve styles the double dealer of his title Maskwell, and describes him explicitly as a villain. When an actual villain rather than a trickster—killjoy rather than playboy—spins the plot, comedy moves perilously close to melodrama. Insofar as it discloses unsuspected malice where we have been led to count upon better behavior, it brings out a hypocritical streak; and hypocrisy, as La Rochefoucauld might have taught us, is vice masking as virtue.

There is psychological significance in the fact that our word *hypocrite* was derived from the Greek *hypokritès*, meaning actor. Truly, the actor leads a double—not to say multiple—life, the key to which is his involvement with his personae. The extent to which he lives those parts may have been overemphasized by proponents of what they term "the Stanislavsky method." The famous paradox of Diderot, in preferring to emphasize a craftsmanlike detachment, would sharpen the argument for the actor's hypocrisy. If he is required to play the role of a hypocrite, like Iago or Richard III, he may even dramatize himself as a comedian, a trickster as much as a villain. He may well find his victim conniving in the imposture, like Orgon with Tartuffe, or Molière's hypochondriacs with their physicians, all of them bearing witness to man's innate capacities for self-deception. In this universe of trickery, the emphasis may shift—as it does in a pair of *commedie erudite*—from the cheats, *Gli Inganni*, to the cheated, *Gli Ingannati*. The shift from fools to knaves turns back upon itself if, by a stroke of poetic justice, the double agent is double-crossed, the duper duped; and then the biggest knave is reduced to the biggest fool.

Dupery is sustained by the shady devices of masking, disguise and concealment. A lover's part would be monotonously straight, if he did not frequently need to gain access to his well-guarded lady. It is not enough for Count Almaviva to pose incognito as Lindor in *Le Barbier de Seville*; he must disguise himself as a drunken soldier to be billeted into Don Bartolo's house, and as a music master to teach Rosine her lessons. Even in *King Lear* the worthy Edgar would be too colorless, if he were not forced into a sequence of disguises. When an interloper is threatened with exposure, he must seek a place to hide—the cruder the funnier, if it happens to be a cask or a chest or a basket or the underside of a bed. Settings can do business as properties here: the slamming doors of Feydeau's hotel rooms or the adjacent houses on the street scenes of New Comedy. Sir Peter Teazle emerges from his closet to behold Lady Teazle behind her toppled screen in *The School for Scandal*. Concealment, in its turn, offers frequent occasion for inadvertent eavesdropping. Shakespeare arranges a veritable quadrille of hiding and overhearing on four distinct planes of awareness in *Love's Labor's Lost*.

When things go wrong in comedy, as in life, they do so for one of two reasons, a mistake or a mishap—or else, and not infrequently, a combination of both. An apparent mishap can really be an engineered mistake, into which the duped can be assisted by the duper. These deviations were indicated by the Latin term *error* in scholarly commentaries, such as that of Lambinus on the *Menaechmi* of Plautus, thereby preparing the way for Shakespeare's *Comedy of Errors*. Such error could be regarded as the comic equivalent of *hamartía* or tragic fault, a slight defect in an otherwise admirable protagonist. The mistakes of Oedipus were compounded by the mishaps that led him into parricide and incest; but those had taken place in the dark and distant past, whereas the tragedy focuses on the train of events that brings them to light. Hence Diderot could have ascribed them to the workings of fate, rather than to human agency. Yet to err, in either genre, whether grandly or frivolously, is to act upon an erroneous supposition. When Ariosto's pioneering *Suppositi* was further pioneered by George Gascoigne's English version, *The Supposes*, the translator spelled out this underlying concept by registering each *suppose* in the margin. Condescendingly and somewhat coyly, the reader was warned:

> But understand, this our Suppose is nothing else but a mistaking, or imagination of one thing for another. For you shall see the master supposed for the servant, the servant for the master; the freeman for a slave, and the bond slave for a freeman; the stranger for a well known friend, and the familiar for a stranger. But what? I suppose that even already you suppose me very fond, that have so simply disclosed unto you the subtleties of these our Supposes; where otherwise, indeed, I suppose you should have heard almost the last of our Supposes before you could have supposed any of them aright.

All of these examples are cases of mistaken identity. There are numerous other ways of inducing a misconception, including love potions and hypnotic spells as well as tactical lies. The ensuing state in the supposer is regularly compared with madness; and the question inevitably arises, amid the conflicting evidence and testimony: "Who is crazy? who is sane?" *Pazzo lui o pazzo lei?* What and whom to believe, in the criss-cross of comic estrangements and false recognitions? Malvolio, deluded into behaving like a madman and impounded by the roisterers that he has tried to silence, undergoes an identity crisis. Nonchalantly straying into the mix-ups of *Twelfth Night*, the bewildered Sebastian is constrained to comment: "Or I am mad, or else this is a dream." Suddenly Illyria has changed into a madhouse, for both the killjoy prisoner and the playboy stranger. Malvolio's discomfiture is prearranged; Sebastian's alienation is largely accidental. On his side, amid unfamiliar surroundings, there is a failure to connect, while those on the other side, misled by delusive similarities, make the wrong connections.

The resulting complication is known as a "switch" in the professional jargon of comedians, and as "bisociation" in Arthur Koestler's analysis of humor, *Insight and Outlook*. At its simplest, on the level of repartee, this can be the merest *double-entendre*. When someone wishes Groucho Marx "a gala day," he replies without the slightest hesitation that he could hardly handle any more than that number. Releasing inhibitions by playing on words, he could take the most innocuous remark and switch its intended meaning to a leering assertion of sex or otherwise a greedy declaration of self-interest. At the level of plot, the switching centers upon the displacement and the replacement of characters. *Box and Cox*, a favorite Victorian curtain-raiser by J. Maddison Morton, adapted from the French, provides an elemental and economical specimen. A parsimonious landlady lodges two as cheaply as one, without their knowing it, by renting the same single room to a journeyman printer by day and a journeyman hatter by night. The lodgers, crossing each other's unavoidable tracks, are foreordained to find out. Before the act has ended, they have also found out that they are brothers, which consoles them both for being jilted by the same repugnant fiancée.

Doubles have been treated so often as singles by farce that a reversal of such treatment constitutes a reduction to absurdity. With deadpan observance of the proprieties, Ionesco presents a couple—apparently meeting as chance acquaintances—who are astonished to discover that each of them has come from the same town, now resides at the same address, occupies the same bedroom, and has a daughter answering to the same description. Their politely banal conversation, peppered with exclamations of *"C'est curieux!"* and *"Quelle coincidence!"*, leads to the mutual admission that they are none other than husband and wife, and have been together all along. The bald soprano of Ionesco's title (*La Cantatrice chauve*) has an absurdist irrelevance to this anti-play (*anti-pièce*); but its middle-class English setting accentuates its burlesque of respectability, predictability, and the convention of oscillating between alternatives. Thus it refers us back to the binary structure of the agon, and to all those misunderstandings, cross-purposes, and *contretemps* which have been so artfully worked up and so artificially resolved.

Much misunderstanding is fairly innocent, and proceeds from ignorance or stupidity. A dramatic fragment of Menander, *The Girl with her Hair Cut Short* (*Perikeiromene*), is introduced by a prologue personifying misapprehension, Agnoia, to alert us lest the heroine be prematurely condemned for kissing a man who turns out to be her own brother. That misguided impression should be considered an accident, though the accidents in literature are purposefully plotted by the author and form a part of his quasi-providential design. The corresponding impact on the characters, if it goes very far, tends to render them irresponsible and to transpose their activities into farce. For Viola and Sebastian in *Twelfth Night* the watchward is "perchance," though the practical joke on Malvolio is blamed by him on the intervention of Jove. The vicissitudes of tragedy, happening in fatalistic patterns, are attributable to the gods or to unfathomed cosmic forces. The ups and downs of comedy occur on the less dignified plane of the gambling table, subject to the hazards of Lady Luck or the caprices of the bitch-goddess Fortuna. However, when the driving force is not external but internal, then cunning reasserts itself over chance, and contrivance gets the better of coincidence.

If *Mandragola* is unique among comedies, as Francesco De Sanctis maintained, it is because Machiavelli leaves nothing to chance. Everything is humanly devised, in a vicious circle of collusion which achieves its end by corrupting the virtuous wife. It is a triumph for *virtù*, in the Machiavellian sense of sheer amoral willpower, the private counterpart of his *Realpolitik*. The resolution is no less unorthodox in keeping the guileful secret, which leaves the cuckold as happy as the rest, and frustrates the ends of poetic justice by avoiding full disclosure. The song that draws the moral could be summed up in Thomas Gray's truism: "Where ignorance is bliss, / 'Tis folly to be wise." If Machiavelli needed a classical precedent for this untypical ending, he could have pointed back to the *Hecyra* of Terence, who has provided so many self-conscious models. There the philandering prodigal asks the courtesan, who has just helped him out of an extramarital scrape, not to tell his father: "*non placet fieri hoc item ut in comoediis, / omnia omnes resciscunt* [I don't want this to be the same as in comedies, where everybody finds out everything]."

More traditional are those recognition scenes which open all eyes, unmask the disguised, reveal what has heretofore been concealed, and dispel the murky shadows with bedazzling illumination. The complications of New Comedy—the Aegean shipwrecks and mercantile adventures, the long-lost foundlings and cast-off mistresses, the broken families suddenly reunited—built up to such an *anagnórisis*. The playwright had to be a little god in his own machine, stretching the long arm of coincidence to round up everybody for a prize-giving ceremony, and relying on such contingencies as a birthmark, Miss Prism's handbag, or the fardel that establishes the royal pedigree of Perdita in *The Winter's Tale*. Plautus devoted an entire play, the *Cistellaria*, to the recovery of an identifying box; the comedy consists of little more than a search for the gimmick to wind up its plot; structurally speaking, the tail is wagging the dog. In *The Comedy of Errors* it is not enough for the Syracusian twin to rediscover his Ephesian brother; as dramaturgic hap would have it, their father must turn up to be rescued from jeopardy of his life; and who should the Abbess be, that affords them all sanctuary, but his missing wife, their mother?

Shakespeare from first to last, from the two Antipholuses to Pericles and Prospero, was preoccupied with the cycle of lost-and-found, the motif of exile and return. Thus his earliest comedy was composed on an elementary Latin model. Since farces flourish on the non-Aristotelian ground of improbability, once we consent to entertain their boggling hypotheses, we must accept what follows as the night the day. At the other extreme from *Mandragola*, everything in *The Comedy of Errors* is relegated to sheer contingency, even to the extent of dropping the sole Plautine character who acts out of self-interest, the Parasite. Shakespeare's response to the *donnée* of twin brothers was to redouble them into a twofold set of typical masters and servants. Here he utilized another hint from Plautus, this time a doorway scene from the *Amphitruo*, where Mercury, in the guise of Amphitryon's servant Sosia, locks out the genuine Sosia—a confrontation which made that name a virtual synonym for *alter ego*. But Mercury had been magically transformed into Sosia's semblance, even as his master Jupiter had taken on the guise of Amphitryon so that he might seduce the general's wife Alcmena, who would give birth to Hercules in the myth.

Consequently, that play was quite uncharacteristic, as the playwright acknowledged; but it is exceptionally interesting in its own right; and it has gone on to inspire so many adaptations that Jean Giraudoux entitled his elegant modern version *Amphitryon 38*. Actually, the total to date was even larger, and included substantial reworkings by Molière and Kleist. Plautus could have claimed no copyright, since he had drawn so much upon Greek originals, deriving his *Bacchides* from a Menandrian prototype that had similarly featured two sisters bearing the same name. He gave that theme an ingenious twist in his *Miles Gloriosus*, when Philocomasium momentarily evades detection by posing as her own twin sister, conveniently living next door. A very different transposition, from self to *Doppelgänger*, would come about in Molière's *Avare*. While the miser Harpagon is loudly and frantically seeking his thief through the darkness, he grasps at a shadow and seizes—whom but himself? His two responding monosyllables, after his cries of "*Voleur!*," seem to voice an unconscious confession: "*C'est moi!*"

After the Menaechmi have finally encountered each other, when one of them wonders who is his opposite number, his brother's pat reply is "*Speculum tuum.*" Each is, in effect, the other's mirror, so that the recognition between the self and the double is reflexive to the point of narcissism. This recurrent trope was acted out through a dexterous sight-gag by Harpo and Groucho Marx in *Duck Soup*. Having seen a live version of the same dumb-show performed by Buster Keaton and a stooge at the Cirque Médrano, I suspect that the basic choreography can be traced far back into the annals of pantomime. An escaping intruder, dressed and made up to look exactly like his aroused pursuer, runs into him face to face. Making believe that he is the latter's mirror image, and that the open doorway between them is a looking-glass, he must fake a reflection by mimicry, duplicating every testing gesture until a false move starts the chase again. An important psychological point has been implied: if you really look into a pair of look-alikes, you may note some difference between them. And when the conformity falls short of perfection, individuality can reassert itself. Tweedledum and Tweedledee agree—to fight a battle.

The plights of twinship always raise a ready Bergsonian laugh. The reduplication of human beings is seen as a reduction to clones, robots, androids, or freaks of nature. This is one reason why militarism poses so vulnerable a target. The army is perceived as turning men into mechanical toys. The sad sack or awkward recruit, invariably out of step, is an easy laughingstock, yes; but, following the wayward march of Good Soldier Schweik, he reaffirms humane values by setting his own pace. Now, a twin is regarded as a kind of human pun, where an imperceptible substitute unexpectedly switches the continuities. Given the interchange of identical bodies and the difference of individual minds, the problems can be projected *ad infinitum* into the metaphysical sphere. When—far from being identical—the twins are of differing sexes, the problem is one of theatrical credibility. By exploiting the Elizabethan convention of boy actors in feminine roles, Shakespeare unquestionably took a stand at a far remove from his latter-day audiences. He prestidigitated in *As You Like It* when Rosalind, while pretending to be Ganymede, pretends moreover to be herself, so that the unwitting Orlando can rehearse his courtship. In other words, a boy-actor plays a girl, who plays a boy, who plays a girl; and the rehearsal becomes a performance—though it was a performance, to be sure, before it became a rehearsal.

There may have been some overtones of transexual irony when Portia appeared as a lawyer in *The Merchant of Venice* or Helena as a physician in *All's Well That Ends Well*. These would come out more conspicuously after women had begun to appear in what came to be known as "breeches parts." But Shakespeare jeopardized the effectiveness of what might otherwise have been his most sparkling comedy, *Twelfth Night*, by hinging it upon a pair of male and female twins. The situation that treats them interchangeably does not avoid an embarrassing dénouement by making Sebastian more eligible for Olivia's hand than Viola would have been. But how could the others have noted no difference between the twain all along? This might not augur well for a happy ending. The ruse of transvestism was employed by Ben Jonson, imitating Pietro Aretino in *Il Marescalco*, to set up a null-and-void marriage in *Epicoene, or The Silent Woman* (where the seldom-used classical title was a pedantic give-away). Cardinal Bibiena, in his *Calandria*, spiced up the *Menaechmi* by changing one twin to a female, then dressing her as a man and her male twin as a woman, and arranging that a husband and his wife should both fall in love with—I forget which of them.

Twins provide the simplest and most obvious embodiment of dramatic duplication, since they invite substitution and misconstruction; but, in themselves, they involve no duplicity, if by that we mean disguising or deliberate misrepresentation. The process of doubling, which they illustrate for us at the least common denominator, is closely linked with a general tendency of the comic dramatis personae to distribute themselves in pairs. This accords symmetrically—and, under the circumstances, economically—with the *duplex argumentum*, the double plot of New Comedy, a precedent for the more elaborate binomials of the Elizabethans. The neatest paradigm is Terence's *Adelphoe*, where a bilateral passage from separation to reunion is conjointly accomplished by two brothers espousing two sisters, helped by two servants and hindered by two sires—one of whom, to clear the incest-barrier, has to be a foster-father. If we are taken aback by such symmetries, Pascal has the explanation: when two faces look alike, we take them seriously just as long as we see them separately; but, when we see them together, the repetition excites our laughter. We are confronted again, from another angle, with the persistent antithesis between tragedy and comedy.

8

ZANYISM

Doubling had its histrionic basis in imitation, which has been the prime mover of drama and of art itself. Its primary exponent has been the zany, or *zanni*, whose sobriquet was a nickname for Giovanni. (There may also have been some link with the Roman mimic, or *sannio*.) He was the clownish underling who, with heavy-handed ineptitude, aped the airs and went through the motions of some more respectable and competent exemplar. This relationship is well described by a Jonsonian simile: "He's like a zany to a tumbler, / That tries tricks after him to make men laugh." As such he can still be the floundering straggler on an acrobatic team. Sometimes he anticipates, as in the Commedia dell' Arte, when a lover is signalling to his lady, and the zany—standing between them—thinks that her signals are beamed at him and reacts accordingly. He is the comedians' comedian, even more than his fellows, since he is particularly committed to the mimicry of their mimesis at large; and a component of zanyism seems vital to the temperament of any good comic actor or actress, since it prompts him or her to enter into a situation and reduce it to a burlesque of itself.

When Volpone plays the mountebank, he addresses his deformed assistant as Zan Fritada. Servants being the principal zanies, it is worth recalling that actors were *servi* in ancient Rome, which meant that they were enslaved. In both Old and New Comedy, the exposition was often entrusted to a dialogue between a pair of slaves, prefiguring the butler and chambermaid of a later day. We are told that the servants of Latin drama were permitted to be clever only in the *fabula palliata*, where the scene was laid in Greece. To admit a *fallax servus* into the *fabula togata* (comedy in Roman dress) would have been flirting with mischief too close to home, since he was so brazenly the *architectus doli*, the contriver of the mischief. Accomplice as well as imitator, he acted as a liaison between the upper and lower levels of the plot. Nor could this catalytic role be reserved for actors, once the actresses had made their appearance: Garrick's *Intriguing Valet* (1741) could meet its match in Fielding's *Lying Chambermaid* (1734). It would never do, but somehow it ultimately did, for the subaltern to become the star. Humbly but indulgently and ubiquitously, he figured as an earthy companion and salty commentator: from the *vidushka* of classic Hindu drama to the *gracioso* of Spain's Golden Age. Knights of the road in picaresque fiction have squires, whose paragon will always be Sancho Panza.

Now a manservant, accompanying his master on adventures which are amorous more often than not, sooner or later finds himself zanily courting a maidservant. Harlequin takes up his perennial flirtation with Columbine. This parallelism was complicated by redoubling and rivalry in Henry Medwall's precursory interlude, *Fulgens and Lucres*. There, while two suitors are paying serious court to Lucretia, their respective servants—specified only by letter—are making farcical overtures to her handmaid, designated Ancilla. The ideological novelty of the plot, which permits a self-made suitor to win out over his patrician rival, is counterpoised by the structural development of the underplot, which follows the conventional practice of parodying the main plot at a lower level. In a normative situation, we would have two couples at two levels in four relationships. This makes a perfect diagram, a square, put together out of those four lines of interplay, two involving courtship and two involving service. Reciprocally, that would mean eight attitudes, and could mean—if it were permissible for love to transcend class—as many as twelve.

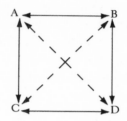

Horizontally viewed, two men are in love with two women (AC, BD); if the women love them, the relations are reciprocal. Vertically, one man serves another (BA) and one woman serves another (DC), and this may instigate another kind of reciprocity. There are two further dual relationships, which can be obliquely suggested, and which could be rendered by diagonals (AD, CB). Such a choreography is set in motion when an employer changes roles with his retainer in order to gain admission into the beloved's household, as Erostrato does in Ariosto's *Suppositi*, sending Dulippo to the university in his place. A similar stratagem furnishes the underplot in *The Taming of the Shrew*; still another brings about an exchange of hats and capes between Leporello and Don Giovanni. All of these maneuvers and innumerable others could point back to an Aristophanic precedent, less romantically motivated, where the role-reversal is between the god Dionysus and his slave Xanthias in *The Frogs*.

Out of such arrangements and rearrangements Marivaux constructed and embellished a tour de force in *Le Jeu de l'amour et du hasard*. Since the title declares that love is a game of chance, we should be prepared for lovers' tactics that take risks, face losses, and arrive at unpredictable consequences. Both Dorante and Silvia have decided, quite independently, to "*jouer ici la même comédie.*" Betrothed and yet unknown to one another, each of them has the same notion of testing one's intended while disguised as one's servant, whereas the two servants are to be disguised as their employers. Each of the principals is thereupon puzzled at finding the pseudo-servant more congenial than the presumptive fiancé(e), while the pair of pseudo-betrothed feel a corresponding affinity. The outcome, duly unscrambled, confirms the *status quo ante*, along with the aristocratic presumption that blood will tell. The gamble turns out to be more predictable than might have been expected, having come teasingly close to crossing class lines without actually rejecting them, and finally attesting the innate superiority of those who happen to occupy the superior ranks.

Judy O'Grady poses no rivalry here for the Colonel's lady. There are a few tense moments when "Harlequin" and Lisette play the *grand seigneur* and the *grande dame* over their temporary inferiors. Yet the social tension is not much more than a syntactic equivocation between the formal *vous* and the *tutoiement*, the intimate or condescending second person singular. As the valet complains, in *L'Epreuve*, *"Toujours des tu et des toi!"* A traditional duty of Marivaux's domestics, in *Les Fausses Confidences* and elsewhere, is to act as marriage-brokers for their betters. But possibly they are behind the times. An older contemporary, Lesage, in *Crispin rival de son maître*, had already shown a *valet de chambre* who all but succeeded—not quite—in winning his master's prospective bride for himself. Lesage had also shown, in *Turcaret*, how successfully such operators could adapt themselves to the new tricks of commercial enterprise. An earlier Crispin, the servant-hero of Regnard's *Légataire universel*, had succeeded in changing a will on his young master's behalf through a series of impersonations, which baffled the notary and the old testator himself, along with the other would-be heirs.

Looking back from the twentieth century to the Commedia dell' Arte, Jacinto Benavente would team up his belated Crispín with an inseparable Leandro, in *Los intereses creados* (*The Bonds of Interest*), as a complementary partnership of perpetual fortune-hunters. As a courtly gentleman, Leandro can indulge in elevated thoughts ("*un gran señor de altos pensamientos*") while the humbler Crispín plies the more degrading tasks ("*el servidor humilde, el de las ruinas obras*"), and is on hand to be conveniently blamed for his supposed master's mistakes. But their interacting is play-acting, or rather—what is not too different—participating in a confidence-game. Nowadays we cannot but observe that the servant-master team has gone the way of the upstairs-downstairs world. From a receding view, in the stories of P. G. Wodehouse, the mood is elegiac if not effete. Jeeves is so perspicuously the last of the gentleman's gentlemen, while Bertie Wooster—so sedately delivered from his playboy scrapes and killjoy aunts—is the chronicler of his own fatuity. The playboys of Evelyn Waugh fight losing battles, and the omnicompetent butler of J. M. Barrie's *Admirable Crichton* is a sentimentalized anachronism.

The turning-point was signalized by Beaumarchais, not in *Le Barbier de Séville*, which started out unsuccessfully as a comic opera, but in the more substantial sequel that so far outshone it, *Le Mariage de Figaro*, nine years afterward and five years before the fall of the Bastille (after a long delay in clearing the censors). Figaro, again with top billing, has meanwhile grown in stature; and it was something of an innovation that a marriage between two servitors should be featured so prominently, though the plot is mainly concerned with obstacles and pitfalls that get in their way. No longer self-employed as barber and part-time factotum, Figaro has reverted to a valet's calling—the lowest rank in a career almost as checkered as Beaumarchais' own, both of them having tried their respective hands as musician, playwright, journalist, speculator, litigant, quack, and jailbird. If Figaro is the cleverest of all clever servants, it is because he has also profited from his author's experience as secret agent, public defender, and subversive freelance. One of Beaumarchais' own adventures would be dramatized, identifying him by name, in Goethe's *Clavigo*.

Comedy was a by-product in Beaumarchais' crowded life, sharpened—as it had been for Machiavelli—by his acquaintance with public affairs. It was merely a youthful hobby for Congreve, who set great store by his amateur standing, in contrast to the theatrical professionalism of Molière and Shakespeare; and it could not have been more than an avocation for an architect like Vanbrugh or a military man like General Burgoyne. Yet Beaumarchais, as a jack of all métiers, had tried his hand at *parades,* skits performed at fairs by strolling comedians. As one who prided himself on keeping up with trends, he practiced and defended *"le genre dramatique sérieux,"* and would complete his Figaro trilogy with an overcomplicated and anticlimactic melodrama. But, as a self-made courtier in a pre-revolutionary epoch, he had found his persona—and the epoch's—in the person of Figaro. And he had raised a disturbing question, at the earlier encounter between Count Almaviva and Figaro in Seville, whether any masters had the proper qualifications for being servants: *"Aux vertus qu'on exige dans un domestique, Votre Excellence connaît-elle de maîtres qui fussent digne d'être valets?"*

However, Almaviva has changed too during the interim between the two comedies, though rather less sympathetically: from romantic suitor to jaded husband. Rusticating at his castle in Spain (a chateau in France would hardly have been allowed under its monarchical regime), this decadent grandee casts a roving seigneurial eye over the nubile maidens within his feudal domain, fondly fastening upon Suzanne, his Countess's waiting-maid and Figaro's betrothed. Complicity between the two women will frustrate his vaunted privilege of anticipating the bridegroom in the marriage bed, but not until Figaro has spoken his mind in a long and devastating fifth-act soliloquy. Now the invidious comparison between himself and his overlord, which has been implicit in their speech and conduct, comes out in a forthright critique. As against Figaro's venturesume autobiographical retrospect (*"maître ici, valet là, selon qu'il plaît à la fortune"*), what has the Count ever done to deserve his position and estate? Merely taken the trouble to be born. It remained for Napoleon to register the contemporary shock: here already was the Revolution (*"C'est déjà la Révolution"*).

With Figaro the servant emerges as hero. If reinforcement was needed for his new standing, it could have been provided by Diderot's contemporaneous novel, *Jacques le fataliste et son maître*. Yet even the Roman prototypes for Jacques and Figaro had obviously been much cleverer than the *adulescentes* whose fortunes they handled. Never was anyone master of a situation more fully than Truffaldino, the most adroit of Carlo Goldoni's Harlequins, in *Il servitore di due padroni*. Serving those two masters keeps him busier than ever, especially since neither must meet the other, and the most important part of his job is to keep them apart (one of them proves, in the interests of romance, to be a mistress in disguise). At an inn, where their chambers are located on stage left and stage right, Truffaldino must serve them both their dinners simultaneously. To have watched Marcello Moretti in the production of the Piccolo Teatro di Milano, alone and almost wordless onstage for a five-minute *cadenza*, staving off impatient calls from both offstage directions, leaping from side to side while catching and balancing heavily loaded trays, was to get a glimpse of what the Commedia dell' Arte must have been like in its heyday.

Instead of the usual one-to-one correspondence between a twosome, we are left with the arithmetical equation that a single servant must be at least as good as two masters. As for his feminine co-worker, the *servetta*, Goldoni promoted her to an innkeeping hostess and universal charmer in *La Locandiera*. There she can see through and show up travelling actressess posing as grande-dames; but, though she is wooed by her titled masculine guests, she prefers to wed a fellow servant. The increasing superiority of the servant class in drama might have been a sign of their decreasing function in society. When every lover had a valet and every lady a maid, high and low comedy were in symmetrical balance. The zany had been the original anti-hero, a reductive deputy for the straight character. Their dialectic was broadened, by Gay's *Beggar's Opera* and its Brechtian modernization, *Die Dreigroschenoper*, into a satirical parallel between the upper class and the underworld. This whole train of development was sublimated by Hegel, and put into a phenomenological perspective, when he envisioned the growth of consciousness as an evolutionary progression from servitude to mastery.

But there could be no falling-off for zanyism in its arena, the theater. Servantless juvenile leads simply had to do their own legwork and dirty work. Lower-class types, such as tramps, received independent attention. The sense of inferiority was transposed from a social to a psychological attitude, and introverted accordingly, so that the modern zany tends to be an insecure little man—a Woody Allen—striving vainly and nervously to meet the demands or live up to the pretensions of a high-pressured lifestyle. Comedy itself has played the zany, whenever institutions were satirized, by exaggerating their claims and limping through their routines. The values of resourcefulness and flexibility stand out against the codes and jargons of legalism. If medicine is more of a mystery, law is more of a conspiracy. The protean and pragmatic Figaro was contrasted with the unadaptable angularity of his judge, the pedantic Brid'oison, whose literal insistence on observances and forms—*"La for-me, voyez-vous, la for-me"*—is contemptuously flouted by everyone else. In the long run, substance prevails over form, and the spirit mitigates the letter.

Comedy had been given some impetus by a group of French law-clerks known as La Basoche, even as London's Inns of Court had figured as cradles for the drama. Since a trial is a verbal agon, it presented an available and dynamic model. An arraignment is the most direct of confrontations; a courtroom scene lends authority to a dramatic resolution. Not that such last judgments are infallible, as Jonson demonstrated in *Volpone*. In *Bartholomew Fair*, where he relaxed his own judicial zeal, it is the would-be reformers—not excluding Justice Overdo—who are condemned to the stocks. Molière's animus against doctors does not seem to have extended to lawyers; yet the dénouement of *Le Misanthrope* is precipitated by lawsuits we merely hear about, which are elaborated into a complex underplot by Wycherley's English adaptation, *The Plain Dealer*. Litigation has outlined many a plot, such

as that of Maître Pathelin's client, who bleated his way to an
unfeed acquittal. Racine's legal comedy, *Les Plaideurs*, imitated
from Aristophanes' *Wasps*, went into the animal kingdom farther
by indicting a delinquent dog and bringing in a litter of puppies
to sway the sympathies of the court.

The juridical type, from the mask of Doctor Graziano in the
Commedia dell' Arte to the wig of the Lord Chancellor in the
Savoy Opera, is more likely to be treated as a figure of fun than
appealed to as a *deus ex machina*. Shakespeare's conception of
the judiciary, whether in Jaques' fifth age of man or on Falstaff's
visit to Gloucestershire, is one which emphasizes human failings. The irony of Kleist's *Zerbrochene Krug* revolves around a
case where the judge is discovered to have been the criminal.
The broken jug itself is the most symbolic clue in a chain of
investigation which leads to the imprint of his club foot. We
might think it a cloven foot and speak of the devil, were it not that
his name is Adam and his potential victim's name is Eva. The
self-incriminating inquiry is carried out, disclosure by disclosure,
in a manner that almost seems to parody *Oedipus Rex*. A contrasting judge, in the rustic interlude of Cervantes, *El juez de los
divorcios*, takes no action whatsoever, but limits himself to
cynical comments on the marital agon, as successive couples
come before him seeking divorce, with exchanges of complaint
and insult.

In those cases where the judge himself must face judgment,
the implication to be drawn is the precept of Christ's Sermon on
the Mount: "Judge not, that ye be not judged." One of the
motives that has animated comedy is a craving for justice,
whether it be roughly or poetically administered. On a personal
basis, this is hard to tell from revenge, since it aims at getting
even against great odds and greater oddities, at setting things
straight where they have been crooked, at exposing plausible
duplicities. At that point we talk about dénouements, which
signify knots that are disentangled, just as the ancients spoke of
désis and *lysis*, binding and loosing. The clarification may prove
all too easy, when the confusion has been so carefully plotted.

The Sermon on the Mount, having admonished us not to judge, goes on to warn us: "With what measure ye mete, it shall be measured to you again." The promised end, that more or less happy ending, is again two-sided in its equipoise. The final audit is *quid pro quo*, tit for tat, *Love for Love* in Congreve's give-and-take, or in Shakespeare's parable:

> Haste still plays haste, and leisure answers leisure;
> Like doth quit like, and Measure still for Measure.

Punishments fit crimes, at least within the comic sphere, and remedies are based on homeopathy. Life itself is seldom so neatly ironic—which is one of the reasons why we go to the theater.

9

DOMESTICITIES

Tolstoy's aphorism about families was an apt premise for *Anna Karenina*, and might well have been the point of departure for many other novels, each of them dealing with unhappiness in a different way. One happy family may resemble another, and therefore—like a happy country—need no history. But when we turn to traditional comedy, we can hardly claim that its unhappy families differ very much among themselves. More of the same is its principle and its program: the mixture as usual. Roman comedies, viewed from a distance, seem to follow the same old plot; and it is "less a form than a formula," according to Northrop Frye. The changing scenarios of the Commedia dell' Arte were enacted by bands of unchanging dramatis personae. Terence, the strategic receiver and transmitter of dramatic traditions, complacently promised the audience of his *Eunuchus* that he would say nothing which had not been said before: "*Nullumst iam dictum quod non sit dictum prius.*" We are distinctly invited, not to behold a brave new world, but to realize how small our shoddy old one is, after all.

It is decidedly not that world expected in *The Tempest* by Miranda, on innocently beholding such "goodly creatures" as the guilty usurper Alonso and the cynical conspirators, Antonio and Sebastian. A sadder and wiser voice is heard in Prospero's wry comment: "'Tis new to thee." Its revelations are those of containment, recurrence, *déjà vu*, the surprise of recognizing the all too familiar. There is an illuminating study of its internal arrangements by E. J. H. Greene, *From Menander to Marivaux*, particularly focussed on the *ancien régime* in France, where the norms seem to have been most strictly observed. Professor Greene's constants are three standard pairs—elders, juniors, servants—and these are often doubled, as we too have seen. Their configuration can be expressed in a symbolic outline resembling the letter F, which perpendicularly represents all three levels, two of them projecting at right angles in parallel complicity, the juniors and servants. The third stands by itself, contracted to represent the elders, who have reached the bottom position by reversal. It would appear that 70 per cent of the French comedies published between 1660 and 1760 are reducible to this paradigmatic initial.

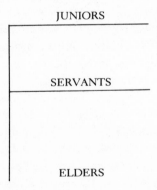

What we call the generation gap seems to have existed ever since a younger generation followed an older one. Shaw is even sharper on this issue than Plautus or Terence. "Parents and children, Tarleton," says Lord Summerhays in *Misalliance*, and Tarleton supplies the predicate: "O the gulf that lies between

them! the impassable, the eternal gulf." Instinctively we sympathize with pleasure-seeking youth, looking through his eyes at
crabbed age, feeling his distrust at whatever stands in the way of
fulfilled desire. An Everyman in a hedonistic morality, suspended between the Money and the Match, he is blocked on one
side and abetted on the other. Inevitably, the agonistic principle
runs counter to the pleasure principle. His relation to his seniors
is negative, despite familial bonds; his relation to the servants is
positive, athwart the social tensions. The former is a killjoy agon,
financially grounded, tending toward satire. The latter is a playboy alliance, sexually animated, leading toward romance. Comedy is compounded of the interaction between the two, varying in
its emphasis from one mode to the other.

It achieved a neo-classic balance in an age when those components could be domesticated within a single household. We witness courtships which depend even more upon the servant's me-
diation than upon the father's permission. Mirabel takes this
specialized service for granted when he cavalierly tells his valet
Waitwell, who is so handily the husband of Millamant's maid
Foible: "Why, you would think you were married for your own
recreation, and not for my convenience." Love, as a source of
motivation, interposes another one of the generic distinctions
between tragedy and comedy: whether the drama moves toward a
death or whether, in Shakespeare's equally portentous phrase,
"the catastrophe is a nuptial" (Don Armado was not predicting
disaster; he was merely indulging in rhetorical terminology). Old
Comedy ended ceremonially, with some sort of *gamos* or wedding rite. New Comedy treated sex as a leading motive, but
mostly on the mercenary plane of courtesans and slave girls. In
the *Casina* of Plautus the titular heroine never appears onstage.
In the *Hecyra* of Terence the title-role is improbably preempted
by a mother-in-law, whose narration and manipulation stand in
for the absent daughter-in-law.

It is worthy of incidental remembrance, as a high-minded
exception to the erotic rule, that the medieval Saxon abbess
Hrotswitha wrote a series of Latin plays on the Terentian model

to promote the virtues of virginity. Normally, however, the comic pattern is that of a mating game or dance. Dr. Johnson outlined the habitual choreography:

> To bring a lover, a lady, and a rival into the fable; to entangle them in contradictory obligations, perplex them with oppositions of interest, and harass them with violence of desires inconsistent with each other; to make them meet in rapture and part in agony; to fill their mouths with hyperbolical joy and outrageous sorrow; to distress them as nothing human ever was distressed; to deliver them as nothing human ever was delivered, is the business of a modern dramatist.

This is a preview, in Johnson's periodic cadences, of the Hollywood master-plan: boy meets girl, boy loses girl, boy gets girl. If it is love that brings them together or parts them, there can be no more than four possible combinations in their reciprocal attitudes, which are expounded by the four debaters in John Heywood's *Play of Love*: the Lover Loved, the Lover not Loved, Loved not Loving, and Neither Loving nor Loved. Their differences were neutralized by the argument: mutual love or non-love is equally fortunate, one-sided love is equally unfortunate on either side. But Heywood's interlude was more of a debate than a play. In order to dramatize the situation, a duo must develop into a triangle, and the rival must be cast in a losing part, if the plot is to fulfil its comic predestination. Though all of Heywood's four positions may be incidentally taken, only the first is acceptable as a conclusion.

Shakespearean comedy, typically, involves a romantic plot with a satiric underplot; in the interpretation of Leo Salingar, it is "essentially a celebration of marriage." Its intricate but conformable design is set by the very first line of A *Midsummer Night's Dream*, when Theseus reminds his ducal bride of their approaching "nuptial hour." That will arrive unimpeded, but disruption will threaten the preexisting marriage of the Fairy King and Queen. As for the quartet of lovers from Athens, both men will have fallen in love with both women, each Jill in turn will be slighted by each Jack, and all four will dance through a kind of

set-to-partners before they are respectively sorted out and defini-
tively paired off. The sylvan setting and the nocturnal timing
intensify both the scramble and the unscrambling. Amid the
interplay of attraction and rejection, natural feelings are eked
out—and mixed up for a while—by Puck's bungling magic. If
we generalized, we should have to conclude that affection runs
close to the surface and that reciprocation is a matter of gambler's
luck. Even in *Romeo and Juliet* new love at first sight cancels out
a prior infatuation.

The disparity between courtship and marriage, as Congreve
marks it in *The Old Bachelor,* is that of a very witty prologue to a
very dull play. The insidious Fainall, in *The Way of the World,*
pinpoints the theme by referring to "the ways of wedlock and this
world." These are far from being identical, and the problem is to
reconcile them. Worldliness does not preclude genuine affection, but curbs the spontaneous expression of it—or rather, de-
flects it into ironic repartee. Mirabell admits but resents his love.
Mistress Millamant barely tolerates it, admits nothing, and refers
to herself impersonally as "one." The Stipulation Scene between
them was well prepared by Shakespeare, with the dialogue between Beatrice and Benedick in *Much Ado About Nothing* or that
between Berowne and Rosaline in *Love's Labor's Lost,* and would
put the finishing touches on many a bout of Restoration banter.
The verbal contract that Congreve's pair works out, their connubial treaty, is a critique of the married state from both sides,
proviso for proviso, measure for measure, love for love. If Millamant is to be "dwindled into a wife" and Mirabell "not beyond
measure enlarged into a husband," then their ideal marriage
should be a perpetual courtship, combining the morals of
wedlock with the manners of flirtation.

Mistress Millamant is characterized—by the affected Witwoud, to be sure—as "a woman and a kind of humorist." If this
is supposed to sound like a contradiction in terms, we might
recall that Congreve, in a printed letter to the critic John Dennis,
had questioned whether a woman could ever be truly humorous—humor being conceived pretty much as uniqueness of

character, if not outright oddity. He seems to have responded to his own challenge by creating Millamant. If she is not unique, she can be compared only to such legendary cynosures as Homer's Helen of Troy or Stendhal's Duchess of Sanseverina, whose charms are reckoned by their impact on trains of admirers. Though she may be the cause of their wit, she is even wittier in herself, thereby providing Meredith with the best illustration for his thesis that the comic spirit presupposes the civilizing presence of womanhood. "Shall we join the ladies, my Lord?" asks Mellefont in *The Double Dealer*. "With all my heart," responds the foppish guest, Lord Froth, thereby sacrificing an extra bottle of champagne, "methinks we are a solitude without them." And thus, when the gentlemen rise at last from the dinner table, the doors are thrown open for drawing-room comedy.

Shakespeare had anticipated the Meredithian posture by drawing Berowne's moral in *Love's Labor's Lost*: that the best books are women's eyes. Dependent as he was upon boys to play feminine roles, he deployed his resourcefulness to the utmost in conceiving so wide a range and so perceptive a presentation of female characters. When his heroines were allowed to dress up in masculine costumes, he was making a virtue of necessity; but that disguise proved to be a liberation from the constraining skirts of the sexual proprieties, metamorphosing those demure young damsels into adventurous playgirls. The tantrums and the taming of his Shrew are crude and early, but already ambivalent, though they are bound to subside into blushing acceptance of man's world. The more resourceful Rosalind, by donning her doublet and hose, can slip away from the restrictions of court to the freedom of the forest, where she dominates the action of *As You Like It*. Shakespeare's Cleopatra, of course, is the ultimate playgirl, and as such can outmatch the playboy Antony. Since they squander empires by their ill-timed gambols, the stuff of comedy becomes high tragedy.

Molière, who could address himself to a sexually desegregated theater, took the fullest advantage of its opportunities to create elegant parts for accomplished actresses. He had graduated from

Italianate farce by poking fun at the affectations of the *pré-cieuses*—a topic to which he would more thoughtfully return. But that gave him the entrée to drawing-rooms where the ladies presided; and, as he ventured farther into domestic interiors, he showed more sympathy for family relations. His women can be affected and capricious, though probably less often than his men; and when male vanity is taken in, it can be shown up by female common sense. The salon is the logical platform for the modish conversations of *Le Misanthrope*, rhythmically patterned by lackeys announcing the callers and pulling up chairs; indeed it becomes the locale for a lady-like wit-combat, when the arch-coquette Célimène and the old maid Arsinoé dispute the respective merits of *la galanterie* and *la pruderie*. Both of the sexes collaborate in the gossip and *médisance*, as they do in *The School for Scandal*; and there Sheridan, like Molière, seems to be satirizing the mode of satire itself.

Shaw would press the dialectic farthest with his categorical insistence that womankind always got the upper hand in the perennial battle of the sexes. After all, what can mere masculine rationalism avail against feminine vitalism? He could point out literary precedents, carefully selected and reinterpreted, arguing that it was Shakespeare's heroines who pursued his heroes, and reversing the legend of Don Juan in *Man and Superman*, where Superman is not a Nietzschean hero but a Shavian heroine of the Nineties—in short, a cross between the then New Woman and *das Ewig-Weibliche*. The shock-value of *Pygmalion* has been outdated, and *My Fair Lady* was faded from its beginning, since there are no longer any verbal taboos for Eliza Doolittle to violate. Although Candida is not breveted like Major Barbara, and Cleopatra is at the other end of the historical spectrum from Saint Joan, all are slight girlish figures who see through the pretenses and get around the obduracies of their clumsy manly interlocutors. Hence they are the spokeswomen for Shaw's own insights and animadversions. Yet his most advanced feminism had long been foreshadowed by the Amazonian housewives of

Aristophanes in the choruses of *Lysistrata*, the *Thesmophor-iozusae*, and the *Ecclesiazusae*.

It is not surprising, in view of the awkward transvestites who impersonated them on the stage, that females should primor-dially have been presented as viragoes, literally mannish crea-tures, or that the sexist bias should have been continued through the distorted persons of dames and dowagers, harlots and har-ridans, shrews and battle-axes, who subsisted to be tamed and thwarted in their eternal agon against the males. The *matrona* in the *Menaechmi* all but drives her husband to the *meretrix*, and he ends by putting her on the auction-block—in striking contrast to her opposite number in the Shakespearean adaptation, the ne-glected and dejected wife Adriana. Noah's Wife, abandoning her Biblical dignity, enlivened the mystery cycles, but was rather hard on her fellow passengers in the ark. Punch and Judy set an all-time example of marital strife, and farces like the anonymous *Tom Tyler and his Wife* or Heywood's *John John, Tib, and Sir John the Priest* vied with the *fabliaux* in their exposures of malice domestic. Unattractive spinsters aggressively searching for hus-bands, like *The Mikado's* Katisha, affright the Savoy Operas. For the comedienne the heavy part is a killjoy.

Men, from their unfairly privileged standpoint, saw them-selves—and theatrical performance generally reflected their im-ages of themselves—as free spirits in continual danger of being trapped and becoming domesticated. It was a part of Millamant's joke to pretend that she enjoyed the option they did, that one was not necessarily destined for the marriage market. Yet there was likewise the possibility that one could have made a better match, which would have been the only viable alternative for her. Un-doubtedly she could have, in mundane terms, and the fact that she does not is the strongest proof of her love for Mirabell. He, on the other hand, as a man of the world, could not be anything but a man of leisure, whose business is pleasure. Forgoing the sole alternative of a soldierly career, he must count his conquests by amatory rather than military reckoning—most immediately by

his affair with Mistress Fainall, a less than gallant twist of the
underplot. Faced with the hazards of idleness and intrigue, how
to be a hero in modern times? Baudelaire's answer was Dandyism, and he defined a dandy as an unemployed hero.

One of the anti-heroes in *Le Mariage de Figaro* finds employment, when the tingling adolescent Chérubin is snatched
away from his puppy-love and sent off to join the army. *"Adieu,
mon petit Chérubin,"* he is admonished by Figaro, *"Tu vas mèn-
er un train de vie bien différent, mon enfant . . ."* Beaumarchais'
prosaic words of practical advice were brilliantly transposed by
the librettist Da Ponte into a lyric—bringing together youth and
maturity, innocence and experience, love and war—for which
Mozart composed Figaro's baritone aria, *"Non più andrai."* It
became a favorite Mozartian melody, to be quoted by the com-
poser in *Don Giovanni* and reworked for a quartet in *Così fan
tutte.* (No more romping, no more hiding, no more dressing up
in women's gowns; instead a uniform, and all that it betokens so
grimly and grandly.) When Figaro changes his tune, in shifting
from the dalliance of the boudoir to the glory of the battlefield,
Cherubino clicks his heels, salutes, and marches off—left, right,
left, right—while a warlike strain swells up from the orchestra
pit, countermanding the butterfly lilt, and the martial music
takes over the comedy with a mock-heroic flourish, as the over-
whelming curtain falls on Act I of *Le nozze di Figaro.* Descend-
ing curtains are spoilsports, brusquely disjoining fantasy from
reality. It is now this cherubic playboy's turn to become a
scapegoat, not to be driven out into the wilderness, but to be
regimented into conformity.

10

DESIGNS
FOR
LIVING

Comedy is never as belligerent as it so frequently threatens to become. Traditionally, its fights have been resolved by feasts. Beginning with the Aristophanic diatribes against war, it has keyed itself to a mock-heroic mode. Echoing his title from the Virgilian epic, Shaw's *Arms and the Man* found its resonance in an operetta, Oscar Straus's *Chocolate Soldier*. Its light-hearted hypothesis, that candy might safely be substituted for ammunition, was exploded soon afterward, when its Balkan locality witnessed the outbreak of the First World War. A posture that had passed for Shavian realism, in a more secure and stable Europe, suddenly collapsed into an old-fashioned romanticism; that satiric weapon had proved too light for the increasingly fearsome onslaught of militarism itself. It would seem that comedy, for all its concessions to romance, is more at home in an atmosphere of mock-romantic disillusionment. When the object is matrimony, the plot is a courtship, and the tone is blithe. When the *donnée* is matrimony, the plot is an adultery, and the tone is cynical.

The transposition stands out if we turn from *Love's Last Shift* by Colley Cibber, wherein the rakish Loveless reforms and gets married, to Sir John Vanbrugh's better-known sequel, *The Relapse, or Virtue in Danger*, wherein Loveless backslides and plays the rake all over again. The sequel was so popular that Sheridan reworked it in A *Trip to Scarborough*; but this can doubtless be passed over as a rear-guard action, reverting from the "sentimental" to what Goldsmith would term "the laughing comedy." The lapse in Count Almaviva's character, from premarital suitor to postmarital philanderer, is one of the many differences in mood and substance between *Le Barbier de Séville* and *Le Mariage de Figaro*. The shadow of the *droit du seigneur*, the feudal presumption that the lord may enjoy a first night with his vassal's bride, hangs heavily over Figaro's marriage to the Countess's maid. Matters are not set right until Suzanne and her mistress (the quondam Rosine) change places to play blindman's buff with the Count, in a nocturnal garden scene, where the errant husband is exposed while trying to seduce his own wife.

This last resort, known in its consummated form as the bed-trick, is similarly utilized by Shakespeare, both in *All's Well That Ends Well* and in *Measure for Measure*. Judy O'Grady and the Colonel's lady prove to be indistinguishable in the dark. Matrimonial jokes seem mainly to be based either internally, on hostility, or externally, on infidelity. If a husband is henpecked by his wife, we are expected to detest her and to sympathize with him. If she deceives him with another man, it is her spouse that we deride; her status, in our eyes, remains ambiguous. When lovely woman stoops to folly, the only decent way out—in accordance with the sexual code reiterated by Goldsmith—is to die (her moral emancipation would be wearily celebrated in T. S. Eliot's parody). In the domestic drama of Thomas Heywood, A *Woman Killed with Kindness*, the husband treats the fallen woman with unorthodox gentleness, but she takes the proper course and expires nonetheless. During the pre-Christian era Plautus could frankly affirm, in his *Mercator*, that a good wife was more easily contented with a single mate than was her husband:

> *Nam uxor contenta est, quae bona est, uno viro.*
> *Qui minus vir una uxore contentus sit.*

Since it was so churlishly a man's world, a woman had no choice but to accept her second-class citizenship under a double standard. She was his subordinate accomplice, whether she was docile or unwilling, legitimate or no better than she should be. Sexuality seems to have been equated with virility, so that the man was free to pursue his amours with impunity—and, in some quarters, with admiration—whereas he became doubly a laughingstock if it was his wife who slept out. There are many explanations, none of them very clear, why the emblem that stigmatized the cuckold should have been a pair of horns. Why the cuckoo's call became a Shakespearean word of fear ("Unpleasing to a married ear") may perhaps be explained by the nesting habits of that vagrant bird, who is invoked as patron saint (San Cocu) of the amoral *Mandragola*. There was a curious mixture of prurience and prudishness in the tendency to look upon cuckoldom as an automatic source of mirth. Yet even the Virgin Mary's consort Joseph, in the mysteries, was not spared some ribald insinuations touching her relationship with the Holy Ghost.

Molière wrote the classic in this field, *George Dandin*, where the misconduct is stimulated—justified, the culprits would say— by a misalliance. The low-born social climber who espoused the faithless aristocrat can do no more than blame himself at the conclusion of each expectable episode: "You asked for it [*Vous l'avez voulu, George Dandin*]." The disparity between the guardian and his ward that invites betrayal in *L'Ecole des femmes* is not class but age, the attempted betrothal of January with May. When the middle-aged Arnolphe undertakes to marry a child-wife Agnès, insulated from worldly wisdom by foolish innocence, her mind is soon contaminated by his jealous suspicions and proprietary maxims into finding out what she has been protected from. Unsurprisingly, this Galatea swerves from her Pygmalion's plans. Her callow preference for cream tarts over parlor games is matched by the culinary trope of the peasant retainer Alain: "*La femme est en effet le potage de l'homme.*" A woman and a wife—the male chauvinism of the French language condenses both into a single word—is not merely a chattel but her husband's dish, to be partaken by him alone.

The counterpart of Agnès in Wycherley's *Country Wife* has been brought up in the same way, with the additional twist that her morbidly possessive husband, Pinchwife, is a reformed libertine. "I will not be a cuckold," he huffs and puffs. "There will be danger in making me a cuckold," This warning is accepted as a challenge by the nonchalant Horner. "Why?" he wonders, and then goes on to ask: "Wast thou not well cured of thy last clap?" Horner's unbridled hedonism will pause at nothing short of personal incapacitation, the only inhibition that he is capable of imagining. But he is enough of a moralist to remind Pinchwife of his own excesses, with an aspersion for Mistress Margery. Horner—his charactonym alerts us—is a dedicated cuckold-maker. To pursue this calling without undue scandal, using a gimmick borrowed by Wycherley from the *Eunuchus* of Terence, he has adopted an extreme camouflage: a reputation for impotence. Nature abhors a cuckold, who is regarded as "a kind of wild beast." But a eunuch is worse, an "unnatural monster," from whom the ladies recoil until they learn that this pseudo-eunuch has sacrificed his repute for the sake of theirs. The imposture is completed with the metaphor of Horner's china, as one by one they are invited to inspect the collection while it lasts—and there are limits, even to his latent capacities. A latter-day pretext of the same sort would be etchings, in those cartoons where a riggish bachelor invites a sweet young thing to his apartment.

The English Restoration was the heyday of the playboy rampant, cutting an extra dash by bearding the Puritan shades in the background. But he could hardly play without partners who shared his commitment to pleasure as a duty; satyrs cannot frolic without nymphs, nor beaux without belles. These had to be other men's wives, of course, not marriageable virgins, and that is where the double standard discriminated most stringently. "The end of marriage now is liberty," Wycherley announced in the epilogue to *Love in a Wood*, "And two are bound to set each other free." *Bound* is a pun, as well as a paradox; the bride is liberated from, as well as by, the groom. But she is still restricted by society's conventions. A gallant may, and must, take the initiative; she must wait for him to offer her an opportunity. "Ah, dear Marwood," sighs the nymphomaniac dowager, Lady Wishfort, "what's integrity to an opportunity?" Such opportunism, though widespread, is not universal; Wycherley is more like Machiavelli than most of his contemporaries in this respect—and far from the example of Don Juan, whose libertinism was punished so spectacularly. The text of *The Way of the World* is preceded by an epigraph from the satires of Horace, suggesting that it might contain a lesson for adulterers, and reminding us of Congreve's didactic stance in his controversy with Collier.

Mandragola and *Volpone* both have heroines who balk at adulteries until their horn-mad husbands are persuaded to collude in their own betrayals, and to insist upon the cuckoldry as a wifely obligation. Both cases were exhibited by a stern playwright as object-lessons in human corruptibility. These cuckolds, being complaisant about it, have advanced to the standing of wittols. The French have a loftier phrase for their condition, *le mari philosophe*, while the Italians speak more functionally of the inconvenient third party, *il terzo incomodo*. Jealousy of sexual rivals would seem to be the more normal reaction, and one of its main components is the cuckold's apprehension of looking foolish. At the tragic level, this consideration does not affect Othello, who is more deeply and sincerely concerned with the vulnerability of his relation to Desdemona. It is the self-conscious question of reputation, the fear of what others might be saying about him, that so distresses Leontes in *The Winter's Tale* or Master Ford in *The Merry Wives of Windsor*. It should go without saying, in these three Shakespearean instances, that the allegations are false.

Traditional relations are reversed when two women dominate a triangle and make overtures to a single man. The masculine protagonist of the unsigned sixteenth-century Italian comedy, *La Venexiana*, is ardently wooed by both a widow and a married woman. No impediments are raised by the absent husband or by anyone else. The only issue is the feminine competition. Such is the happy-go-lucky dilemma of MacHeath, the dashing highwayman in *The Beggar's Opera*: "How happy could I be with either, / Were t'other dear charmer away." This need not imply that all mistresses are alike, since his Polly and his Lucy are charming in different ways; yet it is infuriating to both, precisely because he refuses to differentiate between them. It was left for Noel Coward in *Design for Living* to devise a triangular liaison wherein the lady is married to neither of her constant paramours, who take a bisexual interest in one another. It would seem that her husband—for she has one—is not congenial enough to turn the triangle into a square—if that is the word. Designs for living tend to become increasingly broader, looser, more casually promiscuous. Feydeau signalized the general direction when he entitled a sequence of five one-act plays *Du Mariage au divorce*, and Wilde had his paradox for the occasion: "Divorces are made in heaven."

Love affairs have never been more systematically multiplied or more cynically generalized than in Arthur Schnitzler's *Reigen*. There was no good reason why its English film version should bear the French title *La Ronde*. "Roundelay" is a more or less exact equivalent of the German, originally a dance where each dancer kept passing on to the next partner, with the lurking possibility of an added pun in the third syllable. Ten dialogues are specified by the play's subtitle, more particularly ten rendezvous. This involves ten performers, five of each sex—dramatic equality at last, after so many centuries when the actresses were considerably outnumbered by the actors. These range socially from the Whore to the Count, including the Soldier and the Housemaid, the Poet and the Actress, in a circuit of mobility which carries them upward and downward, completing the chain when one of the penultimate partners reengages one of the first. Two of them are spouses, coming home either before or after their extramarital assignations. The ten case-histories vary enough to be interesting, but not enough to modify the message, which coincides with what Dryden said of the Restoration: "Thy lovers were all untrue."

Schnitzler's swinging round of sexual encounters, with two betrayals for every coupling, is not a *danse macabre*; it is a concatenation of infidelities, not unlike the rebound of rogueries (*"ricochet de fourberies"*) in Lesage's *Turcaret*. These dialogues do not end, then; they simply round another cycle, thus radically diverging from "the catastrophe of the old comedy," which comes so pat for Shakespeare. His finales could have been summed up by the lyric from *Much Ado About Nothing* that begins, "Sigh no more, ladies, sigh no more," and ends: "Converting all your sounds of woe / Into hey nonny nonny." Endings, by a well established convention, aspired to the condition of music. As the concluding song of *Le Mariage de Figaro* would have it, *"Tout finit par des chansons."* But some of those harmonious Shakespearean resolutions could not have taken place without stage-managed interventions. The goddess Diana must descend from a machine to settle the complications of *Pericles, Prince of Troy*. The plotter himself must unwind the plot, if he has strung it too tight. Molière's appeal to outside aid for *Tartuffe* could not easily have been repeated.

Dryden, in his preface to *The Mock-Astrologer*, warns us against expecting too much in the way of poetic justice, on the grounds that vice is bound to thrive in comedy. That is what has happened, more or less, whenever the satiric note has prevailed. In reversion to Wilde's cynicism, values were degraded into prices; and, when everything and everybody were for sale to the highest bidder in a market as open as life itself, men and women were—at least potentially—knaves and whores. They might put on the airs of respectability, as they do in *The Beggar's Opera*: "Knave and whore they call husband and wife." But home-sweet-home might still be a bawdy house, as it had been in the ballade of François Villon, harshly dramatized by Bertolt Brecht and sweetly harmonized by Kurt Weill: *"In dein Bordel wo unser Haushalt war."* Not that such reductions were limited to the underworld, where the guys and dolls were the gangsters and their molls. Brecht's model, Gay's *Beggar's Opera*, had levelled the classes by bringing out the "similitude of manners in high and low life."

When the romantic note prevailed, the ending was really too happy to last beyond the curtain. Tragedy could be more realistic by expecting the worst, and melodrama had to strain credulities in order to avert the casualties resulting from a more dangerous train of events. Happiness could not perpetuate itself without escaping to the never-never-lands of pastoral—or else the un-pathed waters of its maritime version, the piscatory. In the Greek-American film, *Never on Sunday*, the industrious prostitute improves her weekly day of leisure by telling tales to her clientèle. Every one of her stories arrives at the same happy ending: "And they all went to the seashore." But holidays are over all too quickly, and weekdays bring a resumption of business as usual. Comedy, despite its relaxations, despite its recreative origins, ought not to be confused with the sunbathing passivity of an idle vacation. Though it avoids the consequences of more serious drama, it faces the confrontations. There is seldom any lack of troubles to cope with, of anxieties to dispel. Its faculty for smoothing them out has continually been exploited for easygoing and sentimental effects.

The bypaths of escapism generally lead to some sort of rural retreat, although the considered efforts of a Synge or a García Lorca to create a peasant drama were less—and more—than idyllic. Comedy, being primarily an urban manifestation, has tended to stereotype its rustics as hicks and rubes and clodhoppers, not necessarily simple-minded. The country cousin may emerge as the *eíron*, shrewd and sly behind his naive deportment. Such was the original Yankee type, as contrasted with the British, Brother Jonathan in the first American comedy, *The Contrast* by Royall Tyler. Congreve and his fellow sophisticates often made a point of bringing in some awkward homespun booby as a foil for the polished urbanity of their beautiful people. "Ah, rustic, ruder than Gothic," scoffs Mistress Millamant, who abominates the countryside. Insofar as his characters lived by their wits, their agon was repartee—raillery with their own sex and badinage with the other. They maintained their superiority by enforcing a sharp distinction—in Congreve's nomenclature—between Truewit and Witwoud, the former an authorial persona, the latter a pretender who must be put down along with the louts and cullies and other foplings.

Congreve, in spite of his brief essay, was less concerned with humor than with wit, marginally with the comedy of humors, centrally with the comedy of manners. There the dramaturgy is more concerned with dialogue than with characterization, and the style of acting was conventionally denoted as *light* or *genteel*—as distinguished from *low*—*comedy*. "Comedy of manners" is a term which was not introduced until the late eighteenth century, near the decline of its hegemony in both England and France. "Manner" is describable in the dictionary as, among other qualities, "a fashionable air." By aping fashion and pretending to wit, affectation turned manners into mannerisms. In the long run the mannerists proved a worse enemy than the puritanical killjoys, because they made a vulnerable target out of the playboys' lifestyle. Another result was that manners could be treated as superficial and looked upon by romanticists with suspicion. Dr. Johnson could already distinguish them invidiously from morals. Oscar Wilde, in *Lady Windermere's Fan*, would claim precedence for them with a sweeping gesture: "Manners before morals." When Fielding professed to depict not men but manners, not an individual but a species, he was echoing Molière. But Molière's word was *moeurs*, which comprised both concepts.

Manners, divorced from morals, sound frivolous; morals, apart from manners, sound all too dreary. Our sociologists have borrowed the Latin *mores* to carry the full implication in English. Significantly, the French *moraliste* means rather a social observer than an ethical preceptor. "We country persons have no manners at all," complains Mrs. Hardcastle, who longs for London; and the city-country antagonism runs in both directions through Goldsmith's *She Stoops to Conquer*. It reinforces an antithesis between the old-fashioned and the new-fangled, which runs as deep as the inherent conservatism in the Old Comedy of Aristophanes. "I love everything that's old," declares Mr. Hardcastle, who has little use for "the follies of the town," but clings to "Old friends, old times, old manners, old books, old wine." Furthermore, the double standard operates to split the personalities of both sexes. Young Marlow is inclined to be bold enough with common wenches but inhibited with young ladies of his own class. Kate Hardcastle, his unrecognized fiancée, he takes for a barmaid. Stooping to the occasion—if not to folly—she lives up, and alternately down, to both of the roles in which circumstance has cast her.

This reduction to earthiness contrasts revealingly with the similar situation in *Le Jeu de l'amour et du hasard*, where Marivaux's lovers are virtually unaffected by their respective masquerades as domestics. Goldsmith underlines the class distinctions by Kate's very attempt to circumvent them. The mistakes of that night are precipitated by her half-brother, Tony Lumpkin, who is the mischievous kind of country bumpkin. It is he who misleads the newcomers into believing that the manor-house is an inn. This accords well enough with the old squire's disposition to play the genial host, bidding them stand on "no ceremony," and welcoming them into a veritable playground: "This is Liberty Hall." Within an hour it is he who feels himself a stranger. "I no longer know my own house," he confides in an aside. "It's turned all topsy-turvy." How should it be otherwise? And where should playboys be put up, if not at Liberty Hall? It is the comic mandate to turn everything upside down in order that, eventually, it may be put to rights. Without these estrangements and upsets no final understanding could ever be reached. Through such repeated invitations and visitations, we make ourselves at home among the many mansions in the house of comedy. But has that edifice itself become too old-fashioned to dwell in? Has it by now had its day?

11

MIXED
EMOTIONS

The days of Comedy are gone, alas!
    When Congreve's fool could vie with Molière's *bête:*
Society is smoothed to that excess,
That manners hardly differ more than dress.

So lamented Byron in his comic epic, *Don Juan.* He had done
his best and worst to variegate the monotony by adopting the
lifestyle of Dandyism. His playwriting energies were concentrated
on tragedy, and—like the analogous endeavors of so many other
English poets during the nineteenth century—served mainly to
widen the gap between closet drama and popular theatricality.
His admirer Stendhal, not long afterward, made the emphatic
declaration, supported by an essay: *"La Comédie est impossible en
1836."* Comedy was predicated, he argued, on standards of behavior which had been observed under France's *ancien régime*
but had been breaking down during the subsequent years of *em-
bourgeoisement.* Molière, under royal patronage, could intro-

duce *Le Bourgeois gentilhomme* to a courtly audience at the Château de Chambord, which—secure in its snobberies—would deride the parvenu's clumsy efforts to behave like *"les gens de qualité."* Whereas modern spectators would scarcely know when or where to laugh, or why, or at whom. How could they continue to play the game, when its rules were neglected, suspended, or lost?

Certainly distinctions, literary as well as social, had been blurred by the domesticating tastes of the emergent middle class, so that their tradesmen's tragedies were indistinguishable from their lachrymose comedies (*comédies larmoyantes*). But a democratized public might have its own vantage-point. Molière's George Dandin could disclose his predicament as an object-lesson (*"une leçon bien parlante"*) for husbands who had married above their station. Emile Augier and Jules Sandeau, two centuries afterward, could undertake to revenge that situation: *La Revanche de George Dandin* is their subtitle for *Le Gendre de Monsieur Poirier*. Here, with a vengeance, the conjugal plight is reversed; the misalliance is between the daughter of a rich businessman, still the *senex* with his moneybags, and a ne'er-do-well aristocrat who must prove worthy of the match: *"digne d'être bourgeois."* Of course the avenging father-in-law—in effect, the killjoy—triumphs, breaks up the revels, and finds a job for the playboy son-in-law. His holiday is now over; henceforth it will be business for him, however unusual. But the triumph is less than complete, for the tag-line hints that the paternal social climbing will be set back by the Revolution of 1848.

Stendhal, who had died of apoplexy a few years before, had deflected his literary ambitions from the theater to prose fiction, as his fellow novelist Balzac was so exhaustively doing with the *Comédie humaine*. Yet critics had already been waxing nostalgic since the beginning of the eighteenth century. John Dennis had doubted whether the comic spirit had survived the Restoration in England. Goldsmith, even while working toward its revival, complained that it was departing from the stage because humor was more and more absent from life. Hazlitt, the contemporary of Byron and Stendhal, and himself one of the most perceptive theatergoers of their day, asked why there were so few good modern comedies, and answered that they might have become incompatible with the spirit of the age. Manners had been neutralized into conformities. People kept their follies to themselves. Turning from the audience to the genre, he also asserted that comedy might be wearing itself out. In watching the adaptation and reanimation of types and techniques for one century after another, we may wonder whether the process has been slowing down, whether the continuity might not be tapering off at last.

If comedy has been obsolescent for as long as these complaints would attest, yet still alive and by no means inactive, then how must it stand today? Well, the late S. N. Behrman called one of his debonaire plays *No Time for Comedy*, touching this question explicitly and thereby suggesting—I would suppose—the importance of becoming serious, the decline of occasions to celebrate, the dismissal of fun as unwarranted frivolity. We do not talk any more about musical comedies; quite properly we speak of "musicals," dropping a noun outmoded by alterations in tone and subject-matter. And what is so funny, pray, about the so-called "comics," with their blockish depictions of technological fantasy designed to scare the wits out of adolescent readers? As for the "stand-up" comics, those that strike us do not seem very jolly. Even the adjective *gay* has lost its meaning, having been preempted by earnest pressure-groups. One of the best general introductions to drama of the past generation, Francis Fergusson's *Idea of a Theatre*, has significantly little to say about comedy.

Miguel de Unamuno, Renato Poggioli, and more recently George Steiner, have all predicted the death of tragedy, though again it seems a matter of definition; the prediction might be premature. Aristotle felt that comedy had already stopped developing, that it had realized its natural form in the kind he knew. Yet it seems to have been more adaptable and polymorphous than its opposing genre. Tragedy has been more exacting, less flexible, than comedy, which therefore might inherit something from tragedy's suspected demise or debility. Eugène Ionesco has observed that it gets harder and harder to tell the two genres apart. Still he maintains that "the great authors are tragic," while Friedrich Dürrenmatt holds that "comedy alone is suitable for us"—two beliefs which could be reconciled by a rather discouraging syllogism. Both of these playwrights, in ways which differ as much as their respective languages, practise what is loosely known as Black Comedy. It used to be designated "gallows humor," but the mood has broadened as the occasions for it have spread more widely.

"After us, the Savage God!" William Butler Yeats's ejaculation has been echoed from time to time, but with little regard for the circumstances that evoked it. He had attended and applauded the sensational première of Alfred Jarry's histrionic hoax, *Ubu roi*. Not amused but saddened by it, Yeats had commented distrustfully: "For comedy, for objectivity, has displayed its growing powers once more." It is not clear what sort of threat he had sensed in that schoolboy burlesque of French cultural traditions, engaged as he was now in commemorating "the tragic generation" of the Eighteen-nineties. But his reaction seems to have reflected the supposition that comedy had a future, albeit in his view a grim one. For those who cherished the Symbolist ideals of "subtle color and nervous rhythm," this marionette-like performance may have looked like the prologue to a forthcoming pageant of mechanical monsters. Yeats's prophecies could take more optimistic turns; yet the cloud that Père Ubu raised on his horizon may have been closer to science than to an apocalypse, and might have seemed less threatening to more analytic observers.

Such considerations point back to those theories which stress the intellectual, the hostile, and the defensive aspects of laughter. Mankind will never lose the sense of humor that sets it apart from the animals, but the expression of it is bound to vary with the changes in the sociocultural climate. Pirandello envisioned a latter-day version in *L'Umorismo*: "a two-faced sculpture, laughing with one face at the weeping of the other face [*"erma bifronte, che ride per una faccia del pianto della faccia opposta"*]. There the tragic and comic masks conjoin. Despite Boileau's ruling for the exclusion of sighs and tears, even Horace had conceded that Comedy sometimes raised her voice. It had been Plautus who coined the term *tragicomoedia*, but merely by way of apology for a breach of decorum, for having introduced Olympian gods into the bedroom farce of his *Amphitruo*. Typically and controversially, Tasso and Guarini had enlisted the audience's concern, carried it to the brink of tragedy, and then dispelled it with a happy ending. Their stratagems for escape from expectable consequences were facilitated by an Arcadian setting and a pastoral dramatis personae.

Shakespeare's comedies owe much of their mellowness to an increasing component of pastoralism—more precisely, to a strategy of retreating from the intrigues of court to "another part of the forest." Though he was a master of conflation, hybridization, and gallimaufry, he could be as meticulous as Polonius about the *mélange des genres:* "tragical-comical-historical-pastoral." Some of his critics would distinguish "dark" from "sunny" comedies, and would assign his last plays to the separate category of "romances." But the motifs that are instanced to define that synthetic conception—voyaging and adventuring, exile and return, loss and rediscovery, estrangement and reconciliation—figure throughout his comic plays, and are equally important in the earliest (not to mention New Comedy). For all the sunshine of *As You Like It* and *Twelfth Night*, lions endanger the Forest of Arden and mourning casts its gloom on Illyria. It is true that the omnipresent forces of darkness are strongest in certain comedies of the middle period, and it is significant that *Troilus and Cressida* and *Measure for Measure* have had a belated impact during the twentieth century.

With the critical recognition of farce—along with the début of comedietta, burletta, extravaganza, *féerie*, and other lighter forms—comedy proper could be taken more seriously. Christian Grabbe could range through comic modes from jest to deeper meaning within a single play, expressly titled *Scherz, Satire, Ironie und tiefere Bedeutung*. Bernard Shaw could gain acceptance for the problem play by salting his Hyde Park oratory with witty back-talk. Samuel Beckett would classify *Waiting for Godot*, not unconventionally, as a tragicomedy. Ionesco goes a little farther in labelling *Les Chaises "une farce tragique,"* a phrase which Arthur Kopit anglicizes and condenses into "tragifarce." Long before, in concocting "A Tragi-Comi-Pastoral Farce," John Gay had frankly named his hybrid *The What D'ye Call It.* It has indeed proved possible—perhaps advisable—for a Soviet playwright, V. V. Vishnevsky, to produce an *Optimistic Tragedy.* This should do something to offset the trend toward pessimistic comedy. Purity of feeling is a state that can be expressed more aptly through lyrics than through the larger forms that deal with the more complicated relationships. Victor Hugo held that mixed emotions were the defining feature of post-classical drama, particularly when they linked together the grotesque and the sublime.

The point is less well illustrated by his reference to the folktale of Beauty and the Beast—or by the play he was undertaking to justify, his *Cromwell*—than by the dramatic versions of the Don Juan legend. Its originator, Tirso de Molina, was an ecclesiastic, and his *comedia* shudders with reverberations from the sacramental *auto.* It will not be forgotten that this trickster is overwhelmed by his monumental antagonist, and the full billing links them together: *El Burlador de Sevilla y el convidado de piedra.* As with his contemporary, Marlowe's Doctor Faustus, poetic justice drags the erotic playboy into the flames he has flouted. Comparably, the statuesque killjoy, the ghostly banqueter in *Le Festin de pierre*, is featured to outbalance Molière's Dom Juan, who is less of a tricky seducer than a freethinker and philosophical libertine. The ultimate pronouncement there, at the edge of the fiery pit, is that of Sganarelle, the simple-minded servingman who has not been paid for his services: *"Mes gages! Mes gages!"* Verily, the wages of sin is death. The Da Ponte-Mozart title does not mention the Stone Guest, but it morally underscores the sulphurous retribution: *Il dissoluto punito, o sia Il Don Giovanni.* The description that follows, nonetheless, terms the opera a *dramma giocoso* (jocose) or *buffo* (clownish).

Theatrical experience, at its most effective, will run through a gamut of feelings. Under those conditions where a performance has consisted of more than one play, programs have been generally built upon emotional contrasts. Tragedies were rounded out with satyr-plays by the Greeks, and with jigs (song-and-dance skits) by the Elizabethans. Tragical finales were comically relieved by afterpieces and olios (variety-shows in which the actors strained their versatile energies to cheer up their grieving audiences). Thus, at New York's pioneering theater on Nassau Street in 1753, a Mr. Rigby, who had just been slain as Richard III, revived and reappeared as a jovial coachman in a ballad-farce, *The Devil to Pay*. The inner tension between the actor's persona and his offstage personality has been embodied in the archetypal image of the melancholy clown, who must go onstage and draw laughs while his heart is breaking over some private misery: witness Leoncavallo's *Pagliacci*, Andreyev's *He Who Gets Slapped*, John Osborne's *Entertainer*, Charlie Chaplin's *Limelight*. The incongruity between the glamor of footlights and the makeshifts of backstage has become the most banal of seriocomic themes.

In its continued endeavor to convey a sense of reality, the drama is continually exposing the artificiality of its means. Plautus' characters love to step out of their parts and chat with the spectators. Molière takes us behind the scenes in his carefully composed improvisation, *L'Impromptu de Versailles*, which— after a rehearsal that fills us in on the gossip of the wings (*les coulisses*)—ends with the three portentous knocks that usually announce the curtain's rise. Skeptical viewers of *Twelfth Night* must be disarmed when Fabian tells his fellow actors: "If this were play'd upon a stage now, I could condemn it as an improbable fiction." The line is, if nothing else, a testimonial to Shakespeare's control of his medium. Plays-within-plays, by deliberately exaggerating their inherent staginess, increase the credibility of those players who stand by and watch them: compare the stilted rhymes of the Player King with the limpid blank verse of Hamlet. Yet Shakespeare risked too much when he permitted

Lear's Fool to confide: "This prophecy shall Merlin make, for I live before his time."

Comedies have been employed as vehicles of dramatic criticism, notably in Aristophanes' *Frogs* or Corneille's *Illusion comique*. The English theater, in particular, has enjoyed the diversion of parodying itself: with Beaumont's *Knight of the Burning Pestle*, Buckingham's *Rehearsal*, Fielding's *Tom Thumb the Great*, Shaw's *Fanny's First Play*, and the travesties of Tom Stoppard. Englishmen have always been suspicious of opera as a foreign and unnatural species of entertainment. As a rich man's plaything, it was mocked by Gay's paradox of a poor man's, a *Beggar's Opera*. The Savoy Operas were, more pointedly, anti-operas. Both collaborators were prolific, highly competent, and somewhat derivative craftsmen, aspiring beyond their reach—sad clowns, like Jack Point in *The Yeomen of the Guard*—when they devoted themselves to more ambitious projects. Neither, operating on his own, showed much originality. Without Gilbert, Sullivan's songs would have been merely tuneful; without Sullivan, Gilbert's lyrics would have been merely facetious. It was their collaboration that heightened pastiche into parody, clever mimicry into delightful mockery, which might have been satire if not for the sentimentality.

The received metaphor of the world as a stage, *theatrum mundi*, came to life again in the modern theater, proceeding to cross—and gradually to abolish—the footlights, to involve the spectator more directly, and incidentally to question the very fabric of commonplace actuality. We look upon Luigi Pirandello as the laureate of this self-conscious theatricalism. To be sure, it was a ruse of the author's to assume that his six characters led an autonomous existence, antedating their encounter with him or his histrionic surrogate. But that hypothesis enabled him to press those larger questions of identity, ambiguity, and contingency which previous comedies had taken for granted, rather than probed. Other and more compliant characters, who play up to their master's madness in *Enrico Quarto*, foster the impression that everyone is engaged in acting out someone else's fantasies, if not his own. *Cosí è, se vi para*—literally, *Thus It Is, If It Seems So;* more freely, everything is subjective. More objectively, and hence more theatrically, everybody is role-playing. Subjectivity is not easy to dramatize: yet Harold Pinter has adapted Proust for television; and his own plays bring out, with peculiar insight, the enigmatic element in the most ordinary human relations.

In this shifting light, the most dependable attribute of comedy is jeopardized: if not the happy ending, then at least the predictable outcome. Surprises will have been expected all along, if only because the playwright has built them in; but predictability has been yielding to indeterminacy, even in some cases to alternative endings. More and more we learn to expect the unexpected, to heed the admonition of Shaw's oracular waiter: *You Never Can Tell.* When we look back at the comedies of the past, their characterization seems to have been stylized into caricature. The more things changed, the more the people turned out to be the same. That may be why Goldoni believed that all comedy is sooner or later outdated. But Goldoni went on to reform the Commedia dell' Arte by moderating its dependence on plot (*commedia a soggetto*) with a deepening interest in the nuances of character. Corneille had prided himself upon the success of his first play, the comic *Mélite,* because—he said—it had elicited laughter while avoiding the use of stock personages. Even the ancients had recognized a choice between the *comoedia motoria* (fast-moving) and the *comoedia stataria* (stationary), tending toward a stasis which allowed Terence room to linger over personalities and sentiments.

Henry James proposed a theoretical equipoise, when he inquired rhetorically: "What is character but the determination of incident? What is incident but the illustration of character?" Practice, however, has fluctuated between one pole and the other: at the extreme of plot a faceless farce, at the extreme of character a psychological study. James himself, who is better remembered for portraiture than for incident, was notoriously unsuccessful in the theater. We may view his experiments more sympathetically when we note the extent to which drama was moving toward a more novelistic approach. An increasing complexity, not so much in human nature as in writers' and readers' perceptions of it, made it more difficult to dramatize without opening up the available forms and multiplying the exceptions to established rules. Genres at most are helpful classifications, norms to be transcended by the more original and interesting practitioners. By missing this point, the neo-classicists missed a good deal of Shakespeare. If I go on to speak of metacomedy, I am not proposing a novel category, but simply a realization that certain works outgrow the matrix where they were generated and go on to challenge our preconceptions. Genres survive by meeting the conditions that reshape them.

12

METACOMEDY

Hazlitt claimed that Molière was as great an artist as Shakespeare, probably even greater in the sphere of comedy, where Shakespeare was often too good-natured to thrust the argument home or to crush the opposition vindictively. There is not much point in bandying value-judgments at that superlative level, and it would be an odd defense of Shakespeare to urge that he too had his share of malice. It would be more tempting to argue that Molière was by no means lacking in sympathy, which would bring the two together again on the high plane where they both belong. Hazlitt's judgment was based upon the time-honored and somewhat one-sided concept of derision, the dynamic of satire. I have been suggesting that this is complemented, and sometimes preceded, by an element of playfulness, the impetus for romance. It is also possible, as Jonson found, to overleap the comic limits by pushing too far in the satirical direction. Laughter being a social manifestation, nothing could be more suspect or less congenial than laughing by oneself at a joke that amuses nobody else.

Both Molière and Shakespeare lived for about the same span of years; both of them produced a dramatic repertory of about the same size. Admittedly, Shakespeare ranges more widely and deeply. Yet Molière, within a three-year period at the height of his crowded career, wrote three works that stand together and apart from the rest for a note of seriousness, which pervades one of them and strongly affects the other two. They differ too much from one another to be considered a trilogy. Critics tend to talk, in discussing such drama, about problem plays or dark comedies. This may be our warrant for talking about metacomedies. All three of them were beleaguered with controversy. Production of *Tartuffe* was held up for five years, and *Dom Juan* was rejected by a scandalized public, in both cases on religious grounds: the first for its critique of sanctimonious hypocrisy, the second for its expression of skeptical epicureanism. More subtly and ambiguously, *Le Misanthrope* opened up an unending critical debate, and became the centerpiece of Rousseau's campaign against the theater itself.

Meredith may have put a finger on Rousseau's personal animus when he referred to Alceste as "a Jean-Jacques of the court." Jean-Jacques Rousseau may have felt anticipated by Molière's protagonist, in criticizing the worldly values of an aristocracy which was more punctilious in its etiquette than in its ethics. As a devout agelast, he believed that it was debasing to laugh off such a critique. Not urbanely amused but sincerely outraged, Alceste takes an anti-comic attitude, which makes him a suitable target for fun-making. Goethe, who admired the play immensely, commented on the ambivalence of the reactions it aroused, which brought it to the borders of tragedy. Molière had taken pains to balance the issue in the dialogues between his high-minded moralist and the sensible confidant or *raisonneur*, the man of the world, Philinte. He had fledged out his satiric plot with some romantic interest by confronting his immovable object with an irresistible force. It was radical enough that the hero should be cast as a killjoy, but even more so that he should fall in love with a playgirl, who personifies the hypocritical way of life he deplores in all its flattering airs and gracious insincerities.

Célimène is a young widow, beautiful and brilliant, spoiled

and fickle, used to getting her way and getting away with anything. She is also a kind of satirist, though her mode—as opposed
to the virtuous indignation of Alceste's plain-speaking—is sophisticated gossip and elegant back-biting. He may feel some moral
justification when the railleries of her salon bring her embarrass-
ment, though not final discomfiture. But he is forced, by his
anti-social commitment, to be his own scapegoat and condemn
himself to a solitary retreat. Unlike Tartuffe, he is genuinely
sincere, refusing to wear any mask. His misanthropy is the logical
alternative to that cynical acceptance of worldliness which has
been the premise for so much comedy, and his withdrawal from
society reopens the fissure between manners and morals. Ironically Molière, who ridiculed cuckolds and doctors, was troubled
with an unfaithful wife and would be fatally stricken while playing the hypochondriac in *Le Malade imaginaire*. May it not have
given *Le Misanthrope* its unique and problematic resonance that
it was written while he was under attack for attacking hypocrites
in *Tartuffe?*

If Molière came close to tragedy with *Le Misanthrope*, Shakespeare fell somewhat short of it with his portrait of a mis-
anthropist, *Timon of Athens*. It is just too hard to recognize the
extravagant host of the first two acts in the snarling curmudgeon
of the last two, to see the playboy born again as a killjoy, while
the climactic gesture of Act III—the embittered expulsion of his
freeloading guests—marks but does not explain the transformation. Perhaps good nature is at fault again, in failing to live up to
so uncongenial a theme. This is not a problem for *Look Back in
Anger*, which—moving on with its times—has left the banquet-
hall and the drawing-room for the ambience of the kitchen-sink.
John Osborne has inverted the protocol of New Comedy, where
the sire is traditionally irate and the scion is all too easygoing;
indeed his upper-class father-in-law is quite bland. It is the rail-
ing son-in-law, Jimmy Porter, who voices discontent for a whole
generation of angry young men, educated and articulate beyond
their social opportunities. If he is a misfit like Alceste, he would
project the blame on the postwar world of our mid-century.

Jimmy Porter's tirades have already dated, even as his historic moment has passed. The dramatist who addresses himself to contemporary history should bring to it an ironic sense of transition, as when Chekhov saluted a progressive future through the rhapsodic speech of the professional student Trofimov, in the second act of *The Cherry Orchard*. Usually this play has been interpreted as an elegy, an exercise in nostalgia; actually it was labelled "a comedy" by the playwright, as was *The Seagull*, which included a suicide. The late Lillian Hellman brought her own sharpness to bear on *The Cherry Orchard* when she added "a sharp comedy." We should not forget that Chekhov began as a journalistic humorist, or that his earliest theatrical pieces had been one-act farces. As a practising—not a stage—physician, he had compassion, but likewise clinical insight. He was not sentimental, though many of his characters are, each of them caught in the web of another illusion. He was not lamenting the good old days, but saying goodbye to all that, in the bittersweet mood of the twilit garden scene, where the silence is suddenly broken by a twang which sounds like a distant harpstring, mournfully dying away. In other plays it is a pistol-shot that temporarily breaks through the inertia.

In a letter he had promised that this new piece (which was to be his very last) would be funny; it would be "not a drama but a comedy, in places almost a farce." In his absence from the rehearsals of the Moscow Art Theater, hospitalized at Yalta with what proved to be a terminal illness, he failed to reckon with his actor-manager, Konstantin Stanislavsky, who shifted the center of gravity by casting himself as the ruined landlord, the dreamy Gaev, instead of the part written for him, the self-made purchaser, the awkward Lopakhin. With a text as lyrically sensitive as Chekhov's to subjective points of view, that shift tilted the play toward a nostalgic interpretation, more preoccupied with reliving the past than with confronting the present. The homecoming party that gathers to receive news of the crucial auction, with its Jewish musicians, its card tricks, and its slapstick tumble downstairs, is a fitting celebration of anticlimax—not so much a house-warming as a house-chilling. The long-awaited proposal goes unmade, even as so much of the potential conversation goes unsaid. We learn to listen between the lines.

Harold Pinter would exploit this mood of unspokenness, letting the inarticulate speak for itself through his long-drawn-out pauses. Shaw acknowledged a Chekhovian debt, more specifically to *The Cherry Orchard*, when he characterized his *Heartbreak House* as *A Fantasia in the Russian Manner on English Themes*. In both plays the setting is the subject, and each abode stands for the national culture sheltered there during a precarious interlude—an introspective lull for Chekhov, a sudden explosion for Shaw. The latter's ship-like mansion becomes an allegorical *Narrenschiff*, harboring a weekend assemblage of intellectual types, who escape unscathed but not untested from a bombing in the First World War. There is very little action at Chekhov's country estate when it changes hands, except for the pivotal movement of arrival and departure. Yet that departure is conclusive in its gesture of farewell, and the movement is as fluid as in a novel. Chekhov was not a novelist only because he could imply so much in a shorter story. But his dramas also disclose a feeling for atmospheric detail, along with a novelist's grasp of psychological nuance.

Twentieth-century drama took a further step toward narration, less novelistic than "epical," with Bertolt Brecht. Brecht has been a powerful and didactic agitator both for his Marxist ideology and for his own distinctive dramaturgy—and *epic* is a catchword that need not be relinquished to Hollywood. What he apparently wanted to emphasize was a more outward, episodic, and far-flung approach, in reaction from the emotional close-ups of tragedy. But, as his cogent apologist, Eric Bentley, has pointed out: "The new-fangled notion of Epic Theater can be construed as a synonym for traditional comedy." Thus the wheel has come full circle, returning via Brecht's much-propagandized *Verfremdungseffekt*, or esthetic estrangement, to the old-fashioned notion of comic detachment. This may conceivably be that Savage God whose coming Yeats deplored, when he equated comedy with objectivity. Distance is not only a key to Brecht's characters, often harsh and repellent as well as picturesque, but likewise a feature of his subjects, which have been transposed and adapted from a wide range in time and space. To cite one locale: an exotic Chicago, read about and not yet visited, furnished a fictitious background with its stockyards for the legendary Joan of Arc and with its underworld for the Shakespearean Richard III (in the updated disguise of the gangster Arturo Ui).

Piercingly vocal and tireless in his experimentation, Brecht has rejected theatrical realism decisively, seeking fresh inspiration from cabaret, balladry, silent film, Oriental theater, and a good many other sources, both literary and popular. Between the intertextual fullness of his writing and the bleak minimalism of Samuel Beckett's, the contrast could hardly be more startling. From an ideological standpoint, no writer could be more thoroughly disengaged than the latter, whose alienation passes beyond the political and the social to the ethical and the cosmic. Nor would this gallicized Irishman fit in very comfortably with that high-spirited band of his compatriots who have contributed so much gaiety to the mainstream of English drama, from Sheridan and Goldsmith to Wilde and Shaw. Yet he continues to view life, wittily if cheerlessly, *sub specie comoediae*; and his typical spokesmen, however doleful, are seedy comedians trading apocalyptic wisecracks. The object of their game in *Waiting for Godot* is an unkept appointment: endless temporizing, gradual stagnation, unfulfilled suspense. "Nothing happens," complains Estragon with good reason, "nobody comes, nobody goes, it's awful!"

Endgame makes explicit the dénouement that the earlier team might well have been waiting for: nothing less than doomsday. The principal voice of doom is the blind arch-killjoy Hamm, who might be a blighted reincarnation of Hamlet or else—more comically—a ham actor. His dying parents, Nagg and Nell, are living debris, already consigned to a starkly symmetrical pair of rubbish-cans. Clov, his long-suffering slave (and Beckett has restored slavery as both a comic motif and a *modus vivendi*), begins by announcing: "Finished, it's finished, it must be nearly finished." Hamm's continuing jeremiads recall a certain friend of his, a mad artist, who looked out from his asylum window and saw—not the fields nor the ships nor "all that loveliness"—nothing, nothing but ashes. "It appears," adds Hamm, who might be speaking for or about his creator, "that the case is . . . was not so . . . unusual." More unusual, for Beckett, is the remorselessly cheerful chatter of the middle-aged housewife Winnie in *Happy Days*, even as she sinks downward into the earth, and her husband Willie retires to his hole in the ground. "Another happy day" is the grimmest of tag-lines, short of death itself.

We have travelled a long way from those halcyon days when comedy set out in pursuit of happiness. That desirable goal could never have been attained without overcoming blocks, encountering frauds or frustrations, and dealing with them through reductive means. With Beckett the means has become the end: everything seems reducible to its nihilistic minimum, and there is little or nothing to which we can look forward. Prometheus, when immobilized more sternly than Nagg or Nell, could at least draw consolation from the dignity of his cause. Betrothal was the happiest of endings because it promised renewal. Though Benedick put up some resistance to it in *Much Ado About Nothing*, his wry acceptance was justified by an ambiguous moral: "For man is a giddy thing, and this is my conclusion." The generalization is broad enough to suit all moods of comic closure, from Shakespeare to Beckett. But Shakespeare considers the problem most directly in *The Tempest*, when Prospero deliberately breaks off the masque-within-the-masque. When the revels have ended, what is left? The pageant will fade away with the spirits who acted it, and so shall we who have watched it. "The great Globe itself" is Shakespeare's playhouse as well as his world, both the constructs of imagination. If life itself is a dream, dream engenders drama.

Hence in the making of comedies there is no end-game, and the slogan "theater of the absurd" is almost redundant. Even the stalest jokes and most worn-out tricks can provide material for prospective dramatists. Ionesco's elderly couple in *Les Chaises*, before they jump from their amphitheater-lighthouse into the sea, go through the motions of setting up imaginary chairs for the invisible spectators at the non-performance of a deaf-mute orator. How, then, is that message to be received? Reduction to absurdity implies the preexistence of meaning, just as reduction to folly presupposes the attainment of wisdom. The processes of disillusionment never terminate in a revelation of complete enlightenment; they go on and on through the shadows, with flashes here and there. Once we suspend our disbelief, we may find ourselves swept along toward the conclusion of Benavente's *Intereses creados*: "that not everything in farce is farcical, that there is now something divine in our life which is true and eternal, and which cannot end when the farce ends [*que no todo es farsa en la farsa; que hoy algo divina en nuestra vida que es verdad y es eterna, y no puede acabar cuando la farsa acaba*]."

The age in which we live makes it increasingly difficult not to become a millenarian. But, happily, Beckett's muted apocalypse, where grotesquerie leaves no room for sublimity, is not the only millennium in sight. Thornton Wilder's *Skin of Our Teeth*, inspired by the domestic cycle of James Joyce's *Finnegans Wake*, alleviates the vision of chaos and anarchy with a hope for survival and continuity. Believing in "the theater's power to raise the exhibited material into the realm of idea and type and universal," Wilder attempted to modernize the morality play by localizing its abstraction and vernacularizing its timelessness. Ninety years of family living are compressed into the single act of *The Long Christmas Dinner*. Another model family, in *The Happy Journey to Trenton and Camden*, takes no more than twenty minutes to cover seventy miles. In *Our Town* the daily routines of an ordinary New England village are consecrated by its rites of passage: a courtship, a wedding, a funeral. *The Skin of Our Teeth* is a recapitulation of universal history, prehistory, and posthistory, as relived through the successes and setbacks of the Antrobus family, the dynasty of *anthropos*, the human animal.

Many of these later metacomedies, while paying due attention to the formalities of the dramatic medium, have cultivated informal relations with their audiences, eliminating the drop curtain, striking the box set, and supplanting the angularity of the proscenium with the roundness of the original dancing-place. Dance itself, with music and even verse, had for too long been regarded as a distracting embellishment. Comedy's traditional commitment to imitate nature had not really aimed at naturalistic illusion, the slice of life, the voyeuristic room on the other side of the non-existent fourth wall. Its art has never called for the concealment of artifice. On the contrary, it always revelled in exaggeration and stylization, conscious makeshift and evident pretense, giving away the show in order to win it back. Representation is not the same thing as exact reproduction, which would be undesirable if attainable. If comedy solves the problems it sets up, answers the questions it asks itself, and clarifies the confusions it brings about, it manages do so somewhat tautologically, by prearrangement and continual recourse to convention—to agreement between the interested parties, pledged in advance and maintained under pressure.

It is convention that more or less arbitrarily stops the play when the banns are cried for the hero and heroine, taking it for granted—as convention exists to do—that they will live happily ever after. To look beyond such self-imposed limitations is to press beyond the pleasure principle through what we have agreed to term the agonistic principle, and toward that broader and darker conception formulated by Freud as the reality principle. In reality we never come to a standstill at the instant that happens to seem most propitious. "We are not free to do so; the sky could fall repeatedly on our heads; and the theater was created primarily to teach us that [*Nous ne sommes pas libre. Et le ciel peut encore nous tomber sur la tête. Et le théâtre est fait pour nous apprendre d'abord cela*]." So, at all events, we have been warned by Antonin Artaud. Can it be then, in the last analysis, that tragedy is truer than comedy, that the avenging killjoys were right all along, and that the capering playboys must sooner or later be put in their place—which was hell for Don Juan, after all? "Is this the prom-is'd end?"

The question was Kent's in *King Lear*, and our response—if it is to be anything more than an echo—must come from science, religion, or philosophy, not from art. The mortal imminence of that falling sky has, for the most part, been the stuff of tragedy. And tragedy still helps to define its opposing visage, though decline has induced it to hand over some of its burdens. With Artaud the old antithesis was fused into a "theater of cruelty," which—if ever fully accepted—would self-destruct. Comedy does offer a measure of freedom, in the form of release from constraints and relief from anxieties; but these benefits, like all pleasures, are temporary. What stays with us is that exhilarating awareness of the better life we never lived. We can get rid of Malvolio, dispatch him out into the wilderness, and go back to Sir Toby's cakes and ale. Yet the apparition of Alceste will continue to haunt us with his misgivings; Prospero, stripped of his magical robes, will discharge our illusions; while Hamm, though eyeless and moribund, will still be alive and kicking. The most protean aspect of comedy is its potentiality for transcending itself, for responding to the conditions of tragedy by laughing in the darkness. Petrushka may shed his sawdust, and his Moorish slayer may run away with the Ballerina; but his clownish ghost will reappear, smiling down irrepressibly on the Showman from the top of the puppet-booth.

SUPPLEMENTARY
ESSAYS

A

FROM
PLAY TO
PLAYS

"Work consists of whatever a body is *obliged* to do," Mark Twain
has written. ". . . Play consists of whatever a body is not obliged
to do." This distinction, as Tom Sawyer learns and lives it, is
what stands between being ordered to whitewash a fence and
allowing other boys—for a consideration—to whitewash that
fence. Comparably, though we might not think of Immanuel
Kant as a prime exponent of the pleasure principle, his esthetics
were based upon the conception of free play, a purely disinterested mode of activity. That autotelic impetus was expressed
more emphatically by his poetic disciple, Friedrich Schiller:
"Man plays only when he is in the fullest sense of the word a
human being, and *he is only a complete human being when he
plays*." Man is a playful if not an entirely rational animal, by
Aristotelian definition the sole animal who laughs. Schiller
speaks of *Spieltrieb*, the play instinct, the urge toward esthetic

pleasure, *Spiel* signifying game and likewise drama in German: *Schauspiel* (show-game), *Trauerspiel* (mourning-game or tragedy), *Lustspiel* (pleasure-game or comedy). We encounter the same double meaning in the English word *play*, as well as in the French *jeu* and the Latin *ludus*. Though there is no parallel in Greek, it is significant that *drama* was derived from a root which means act, another ambiguity. *Play* itself primarily connoted movement or exercise, as in swordplay, and has often been connected with music, as in playing an instrument.

During recent years there has been psychological small-talk about the games that people play. *Game* is etymologically related to concepts of participation and communion. Gamesmanship has been reduced to one-upmanship, the habit of manuevering for personal advantage by appealing to social conventions. But there are times when one must appeal against *les règles du jeu* to life itself, as Alice discovers, waking up from nightmare to reality by telling her adversaries of Wonderland, "You're nothing but a pack of cards!," or alternately pulling out the tablecloth from the banquet of chessmen in *Through the Looking-Glass*. In both conclusive situations the game, in each case a different game, is up. It might well seem that

> Love is a game, poetry is a game, life should become a game (this is the sole hope for our political struggles), and "the revolution itself is a game," as the most conscious among the revolutionists said in May. [So Alain Robbe-Grillet was writing in 1970. Nevertheless, he went on to say:] The rapid recovery from their gesture through moral, humanistic, and ultimately religious values has also shown that our society was not yet quite ready to heed such a watchword . . .

Games have formed a conventional part of the epic, to be sure, and the great mock-epic of Rabelais includes a long catalogue in which we recognize such unheroic sports as dice, cards, checkers, marbles, jackstraws, skittles, tiddledy-winks, shuttlecock— not to mention French counterparts of London Bridge and morris dances. The Russian critic Mikhail Bakhtin has concretely demonstrated the large extent to which the Rabelaisian jests and japes were grounded in the popular customs of the Middle Ages. It should be said that Bakhtin, as a Marxist, emphasizes feasts and fairs and folktales at the expense of Renaissance humanism, which found such eloquent and sardonic expression in the same hodgepodge. But it is precisely the intermixture of broad buffoonery and speculative fantasy that makes *Gargantua* and *Pantagruel* so unique.

The basic seriousness of what might have seemed a frivolous subject was firmly established by the Dutch historian Johan Huizinga in *Homo Ludens: A Study of the Play-Element in Culture*, a comparative sketch of civilization viewed *sub specie ludi.* "Tell me how they played," says Huizinga in effect, "and I can tell you what they were." The mechanism he stresses is the agon, as organized through love or war or other institutions. Such conflict, taking dramatic form, was a central feature in the Old Comedy of Aristophanes, notably the debate between Right Reason and Wrong Reason in *The Clouds*, and it animated the long tradition of New Comedy in its battles of the sexes, generations, and classes. What Huizinga called "the agonistic principle" was not wholly disinterested, insofar as it pitted rival forces in a competition against each other. Medieval prizes could be garnered by wrestling for a ram or climbing a greasy pole for a leg of mutton. Yet, when sport was institutionalized, commercialized, and even politicized, it remained a game, the moral equivalent of warfare. There was a general armistice during the public games that took place at Olympia and elsewhere in Greece under religious auspices. Athletic contests—races on foot or in chariots, throwing the discus or javelin, archery and gymnastics—were supplemented by such skills as flute-playing; and the victors were rewarded not only with garlands, but with choric odes of mythical dimensions by such poets as Pindar.

Happily the losers were not executed, unlike Roman gladiators or Mayan handball players. But whereas the Greeks participated as amateurs, making athletics an integral part of their lifestyle, the Romans professionalized it into a spectator-sport. They brought in the animals, augmented the circuses, flooded the arenas and staged *naumachiae* or miniature sea-battles, and produced such amphitheatrical spectacles as the pageant of Troy, *Ludus Troiae*. Another adumbration of our theme, a book entitled *Les Jeux et les hommes* by Roger Caillois, reminds us that *agón* has coexisted with *alea*, the agonistic with the aleatory, therewith introducing an element of hazard. The fatalism of the Latin proverb, *Jacta est alea* (the die is cast), would be challenged by the indeterminacy of Mallarmé's title and poem, *Un coup de dés jamais n'abolira le hasard* (a cast of the dice will never do away with chance). And though there may be some games of pure chance, luck is a factor in most games of skill, as it is in human destiny, where it can be attributed to the vicissitudes of a sometimes deified Fortune. When destinies are projected by a writer, fictionally or dramatically, it is he who arranges the patterns of irony or coincidence and operates as the god in his own machine. A theory of games has been developed, out of the mathematics of probability, to predict the hazards of economic or military engagement. *Kriegspiel*, however, has yet to be accepted as an exact science.

Another, and perhaps the strongest, component within the ludic impulse is mimicry. Aristotle held that basic motivation in the arts was *mímesis*, the imitation of nature. This had a functional basis so long as men believed in sympathetic magic. Indians upon the Western plains could mime the buffaloes in their preparation for a hunt or engage in rain-dances to dispel the drouth. Dancing has always involved a transference from employment to play. Its configurations have been determined by an additional instinct which Aristotle discerned giving rise to art: *harmonía*, whatever harmony may stand for in that context. The interconnection between dance and drama was sealed by the name that the Greeks gave to their circular playing-area, *orchestra* or dancing-place. It was no accident that, when Henri Bergson analyzed laughter, he chose his examples from children's toys, such as the jack-in-the-box for a reflexive response, or the jumping jack for string-pulling manipulation, or—not a toy but a sport—the snowball for repetition and accumulation. Most playthings, if they were not simple noisemakers or whirligigs of some sort like babies' rattles, have been small-scale models of grown-up paraphernalia. Most children's games, as Herbert Spencer pointed out, are dramatizations of adult activities, going through the motions in make-believe. It is their developmental function, as Jean Piaget has more recently perceived, to help the very young in the process of assimilating realities.

The lilting rounds of "Shall I tell you how the farmer . . . / Sows his barley and his wheat?" imitate rather didactically the chores of agriculture. "The farmer in the dell" goes farther domestically, and—with "The farmer takes a wife"—becomes a kind of mating dance. Similarly, the mock-labors of "Oats and beans and barley grow" move on toward the romantic suspense of "Waiting for a partner." *Pas de deux*, at any level, are bound to be stylizations of courtship: was it not at a ball that Romeo met his Juliet? Yet dancing must be regarded as a communal observance, which links the individual with the surrounding group. "Here we go round the mulberry bush" may indeed preserve, in fossilized simplification, some relics of Druidical tree-worship. Parallels and precedents could be adduced from innumerable cultures, but my examples will be chiefly Anglo-American. If these can be readily and agreeably culled, it is because so much has been done to collect and interpret the folkways of English children, from Joseph Ritson and Joseph Strutt in the eighteenth century to Iona and Peter Opie in our time. The Opies believe that such pastimes are "more akin to ceremonies than to competitions." This is not to assert that they are altogether free from aggression. "King of the Castle" (or "King of the Hill," as it is known in its defeudalized American version) offers a ringing invitation to push and to shove which has been cited as far back as the First Epistle of Horace.

Mother Goose—if not her French foster-sister, Ma Mère de l'Oie—presides over age-old midden-heaps of cultural detritus. "Baa, baa, black sheep" preserves a topical allusion to the medieval wool trade, "The King of France" a jeer at the retreating army of Henry of Navarre. The Lion and the Unicorn salute the uneasy union of England and Scotland. A good many nursery rhymes were originally acted out. "Dipping"—counting-out with such nonsensical numbers as "Eeny, meeny, miny, mo"— serves as a prelude to more active diversions, though there is a dark surmise that the primordial *it* may have been a ceremonial victim. Adults, when playing with infants, dandle them on their knees to the rhythm of "Ride a cock-horse to Banbury Cross" or call the roll of fingers and toes with "This little pig went to market." In both "Pat-a-cake, pat-a-cake" and "Pease porridge hot," hand-clapping sets the pace for culinary concerns. "Roses are red, / Violets are blue" is nothing more nor less than a valentine. "Lady-bird, lady-bird, fly away home" must have once been an incantation, albeit not the most effective method of insect-control. The magical charm, "Rain, rain go away" was a polar opposite to the Indian dance that evoked precipitation. Divination was practised to test a lover by pulling off the petals of a flower ("He loves me, he loves me not") or to look into the future for a career by calling another roll ("Rich man, poor man, beggarman, thief").

Much poetry originated in riddles, primitive metaphors turned into guessing games, which could be amplified through dialectic into dialogue, and elaborated to their highest pitch in the Sophoclean tragedy of *Oedipus the King*. Among more naive exemplars of the enigma, "Humpty Dumpty" seems to be the most widespread, with versions in numerous languages, and the most germinal, possibly because of its obvious answer: an egg. The rhyme and game of "London Bridge" are especially reminiscent of historical and topographical associations. Through its dénouement it is closely associated with "Oranges and Lemons." Both bear a close relationship to another evocation of London's landmarks: "Oranges and lemons, / Say the bells of Saint Clement's." In the choreography of "London Bridge," after the players file through the hand-held arch and it comes down upon the prisoner, the verbal formula suggests a grim sacrifice:

Here comes a candle to light you to bed:
Here comes a chopper to cut off your head.

And after all the marchers have been disposed of as Oranges or Lemons, lining up behind the anchor-men on one side or the other, the ceremony terminates in a tug of war. This team-game had earlier been played with a rope of twisted grain, whose full possession was deemed lucky for the owner's crops. In similar fashion, on Hock-tide or other occasions, the burnt skull of a sacrificed beast was bandied through the streets of northern villages. That became the puck in hockey; and, since there was a taboo against touching it, shepherds' crooks were utilized as sticks. The original objective was home, the player's family garden; but secularization reversed the goal, which became the opponents' cage. Comparable origins have been conjecturally ascribed to soccer, football, and analogous field games. If we assume that supernatural powers were being propitiated for anyone's benefit, then we accept the notion of a more or less utilitarian purpose. Otherwise the triumph is for its own sake, and playfulness flourishes in the decay of belief. "The debris of ritual," in E. K. Chambers' phrase, survives as psychodrama or practical joking.

The painter who most expressly and encyclopedically rendered *homo ludens*, Pieter Breughel, crowded more children's games into a single canvas than anyone could expect to recognize. In another panoramic painting, "The Battle of Carnival and Lent," his agon between good cheer and mortified flesh allegorizes the perennial alternation between the feast and the fast, the seasons of plenty and famine. Rules had been relaxed and routines suspended during the Saturnalia in ancient Rome. These were conceived as a temporary restoration of Saturn's Golden Age: an interim of truce, of closing schools and freeing slaves, of licensed gambling and exchanging gifts. During the Middle Ages the protocol of the church had been playfully interrupted by the Feast of Fools, when choirboys burlesqued the liturgy and misrule was the order of the day. I have mentioned Bakhtin's interpretation of the carnivalesque in Rabelais. How that carnival spirit—with its chartered liberties, its particolored masquerading, its emphasis on food and drink and sex—affected the Elizabethan theater has been vividly shown by C. L. Barber in *Shakespeare's Festive*

Comedy. And Erich Segal, in *Roman Laughter,* has traced the classical comedy of Plautus directly to its Saturnalian matrix. Greek tragedy, as we know, began as a *sacer ludus,* and comedy drew its name from a village revel, *kōmos.* Its eponymous hero, the god of revelry, was Comus, and Milton's puritanical masque might be described as a rout for comedy.

Tragedy led toward a funeral, comedy toward a marriage; if the prospective ceremonies were not literally enacted, at least there were terminal processions. Everything has its season, and the major celebrations could be timed by the rhythms of life and death and the means of subsistence, by the cycle of vegetation with its implicit promises of annual renewal. Its high points had to be the summer and winter solstices: on the one hand, the pristine rites of May Day, currently and piously observed by Marxists at the Red Square in Moscow; on the other, the northern analogue of the Saturnalia, Yuletide. Temporally, these have a rough correspondence with the Christian festivals of Resurrection and Nativity, Easter and Christmas. Holidays originally came into existence as holy days, though some of the most archaic would be denounced as pagan during the Reformation. Here we may recall, from the comprehensive denunciation of Queen Elizabeth's epoch by Philip Stubbes, *The Anatomy of Abuses,* his attack on the raising of the Maypole:

> Against May, Whitsunday, or other time, all the young men and maids, old men and wives, run gadding overnight to the woods, groves, hills, and mountains, where they spend all the night in pleasant pastimes; and in the morning they return, bringing with them birch and branches of trees, to deck their assemblies withal. And no marvel; for there is a great lord present amongst them, as superintendant and lord over their pastimes and sports, namely Satan, Prince of Hell. But the chiefest jewel they bring from thence is their Maypole, which they bring home with great veneration . . .

Stubbes, a zealous spokesman for what Jonas Barish has lately defined as "the antitheatrical prejudice," visualizes Satan as a Lord of Misrule or a Master of the Revels. Yet, when he lingers to detail the flags and kerchiefs of the May-games, their boughs and arbors, and the very nosegays between their oxen's horns, the Puritan pamphleteer betrays the Elizabethan-in-spite-of-himself. He catches himself before he is carried away, to reinforce the moral with prurient statistics:

> Then fall they to dance about it, like as the heathen people did at the dedication of the Idols, whereof this is a perfect pattern, or rather the thing itself. I have heard it credibly reported (and that *viva voce*) by men of great gravity and reputation that of forty, threescore, or a hundred maids going to the wood overnight, there have scarcely the third part of them returned home again undefiled.

This is a far cry from blithe madrigals about Maying, from Shakespeare's vernal excursions or Herrick's Corinna. But always, where there are playboys, there are likely to be killjoys. With genial nostalgia the Anglican bishop Richard Corbet lamented, in "The Fairies' Farewell," that the folklore of Merry England had been losing ground through the rise of Puritanism and the decline of Catholicism ("the old religion").

Each of the two traditional festivities had its characteristic dance. On Christmas or New Year's Day in England and Scotland it was the Sword Dance, a mimetic battle, conceivably the domesticated survival of a bloodier confrontation, darkly intimated when the dancers locked swords around the head of a kneeling clown. In the merry month of May or thereabouts it was the morris dance, so named because of its supposedly Moorish source, though the faces of the performers were probably first blackened by the ashes from some primitive hecatomb. Capering to pipe and tabor, most of them were outfitted with baldrics, bells, and sticks. There was a distinctive outfit for the prancing hobby-horse, whose obsolescence Shakespeare mourned as Corbet would mourn for the fairies. There was also a familiar character known as the Bessy, a man dressed as a woman, who may have had to do so at a ritual stage when matriarchy prevailed. The custom of transvestism, travesty in its literal sense, would survive into the Christmas pantomime, where the "principal boy" or *jeune premier* was a girl in tights and the Widow Twanky or Wicked Witch was a female impersonator. The heroine of spring, like Shakespeare's Perdita, could have been a lineal descendant of the Roman goddess Flora. As Maid Marian, the Lady of May, she presided with the Lord of May, Robin Hood, over the May-games. These embodied the agonistic principle on the plane of athletics: in wrestling, bouts with quarterstaff, and contests of archery.

If the contestant, when challenged, did well against the King of the Wood, the latter blew his horn to summon his merry men and thereupon invited the newcomer to join his little band in Lincoln green. The happy ending of each episode was an initiation into the greenwood of primitivistic companionship. That greenery had more to do with chlorophyll than with Lincolnshire; it came closer to nature than to history. If you remember Scott's *Ivanhoe*, you will call to mind the fictional image of Robin Hood (alias Locksley) as the leader of an Anglo-Saxon underground after the Norman Conquest. This was a novelistic fabrication. Actually *Robin* is the French nickname for *Robert*; Hood is a contraction of the Middle English *à wood* ("of the wood"); and his honorific title, *Earl of Huntington*, merely personifies him as a patron of hunting, a guardian genius of the chase. The legendary outlaw was modelled not upon a historical figure but on a forest sprite. As for Maid Marian, her maidenhood would all too frequently be called into question. In one ballad Robin Hood turns her over to Friar Tuck as "a trull of trust / Fit to serve a friar's lust." More refined was the treatment of the legend dramatized by a troubadour of the thirteenth century, Adam de la Halle. His remains our best example of a peculiar Old French genre, the *pastourelle*, a highly specialized version of pastoral which—like all the others—presented a sophisticated idealization of the simple life: *Le Jeu de Robin et Marion*.

The plot could hardly be simpler. It involves a shepherd, Robin, ultimately united to his shepherdess, Marion, though not before a temporary discomfiture while seeking to protect her from the advances of a wayfaring knight. Then the fellow shepherds and shepherdesses celebrate with songs and dances—and with games, *jeux-entre-jeux* as it were. One of them, involving questions and answers and forfeits, seems to be an anticipation of "Truth or Consequences." Another, *Rois et reines*, grants each of those happy rustics the opportunity to play king or queen for a moment. The homespun English accounts of Robin and belatedly Marian were handed down to us through ballads, mostly subsequent to the fifteenth century. For a more continuous tradition than that of these ingenuous *sacres du printemps*, we must turn to the Christmas mummings, transmitted by word of mouth from an immemorial past well into our twentieth century. We possess well over a thousand redactions, following pretty much the same scenario, with some interesting local variations. Villagers and peasants were the beribboned mummers— often illiterate—proceeding from house to house, giving a performance and taking up a collection under the patronage of Saint George (for Merry England). He is the scheduled protagonist, although not infrequently he turns out to be the agonist. His regular antagonist is not the mythical dragon but rather the Turkish Knight, whose antagonism may be dated historically from the Crusades.

One of the informants, who obviously learned his part by imperfect ear, has rechristened him "the Turkey Snipe," and he has borne such other sobriquets as "Bold Slasher," "Captain Thunderbolt," and "Black Prince of Darkness." In some versions dating from about 1800 the hero is King George, with his adversary updated to a "black and American dog" in one instance and in another to Bold Bonaparte. Lord George appears from time to time, and once—by further modernization—Lloyd George. By conflation, still another contest opposes Robin Hood to Little John. Since most of the scripts have been written down within the last hundred years or so, they are not free from anachronistic intrusions. The play is customarily opened by such well established figures as Father Christmas and Beelzebub; but the file parading through the finale has included such dramatis personae as Donald Duck and Suffragette, along with Old King Cole, King

Alfred, Oliver Cromwell, and Giant Blunderbore; and the final anthem, before the collection is taken, has varied from "The British Grenadiers" to "Yankee Doodle." The tragic movement is invariably reversed: a fall goes before a rise. Hubris, to be sure, has provoked the challenge, the exchange of vaunts and taunts, a verbal agon which resembles the flytings or slanging-matches in Anglo-Saxon and Scottish poetry:

> I'll hash you and smash you as small as flies,
> And send you to Jamaica to make mince pies.

Words then give way to deeds, to a physical combat wherein one or another of the combatants gets killed. Now it is Saint George, and again the Turkish Knight, under a Manichean dispensation which is not concerned to stack the odds between heroism and villany. After all, there is no need to dread the outcome. Among the stage directions at this peripety, we find "one will fall"—and even "all fall down," which directs us back toward the realm of child's play.

This is the tragic lull before the restorative climax. Enter the Doctor with his clinical assistant commonly styled Jack, who brings in a hammer, a saw, and other surgical instruments, while his master trumpets their professional claims:

> I can cure the itch, the stitch, the palsy, and the gout,
> Pains within and pains without . . .

And the Doctor rattles on with what would later be termed a pitch—or, more significantly from our viewpoint, a *Spiel*. Like the vein of the charlatan in a medicine show, sugarcoating the nostrums he vends with snatches of entertainment, it reverberates into the mountebank scene of Ben Jonson's *Volpone* and the song of the Opérateur in Molière's *Amour médecin*. Jack introduces himself in a scrambled lingo of his own: e.g., "I met a bark and he dogged at me." He engages in horseplay with the Doctor; with exaggerated effort they jointly manage to extract an enormous property tooth, actually drawn from a horse or a cow. When that business works no cure, a medicinal herb is administered, normally elecampane. It proves just as ineffectual, even when misreading by rote gives us "elegant paint" in one textual variant, or in another—most elegantly—"champagne." Whereupon the medicine man renounces all medicaments in favor of a more potent remedy:

> I torture not my patient with excations
> Such as pills and embrocations,
> But by a word of command
> I can make this mighty prince to stand.

And he revives the prostrate champion by pronouncing the word of command: "Arise!" I shall not pause to suspect a *double-entendre* at this point. At this point the charlatan himself is metamorphosed into a shaman, the priestly celebrant in a liturgical drama of death and revival as it has been performed by the cults of Osiris, Adonis, and Baldur, all of them avatars of the dying god who reenacts a myth of resurrection. Where crucifixion would consummate a tragedy of tragedies, resurrection transposes it into a Divine Comedy. Its Christian manifestation is the Easter trope of the church, with the empty sepulcher and the angel's announcement that Christ has arisen: "*Surrexit. Non est hic . . .*"

The Mummers' Plays show signs of having been rooted in pre-Christian observance, though they have been collected through their survival into the past two centuries. Thomas Hardy has provided us with a lively account of a performance in *The Return of the Native*. It is a typical escapade for his headstrong Eustacia Vye to disguise herself and appear with the mummers: and it was utterly atypical for them, in view of their unliberated assumption that women sewed the costumes and men did the performing. Elsewhere, in *The Mayor of Casterbridge*, Hardy, whose roots went so deep into the lore of his native Dorset, has touched upon another rural custom, the "skimmity-ride." Riding the skimmington, as it was more formally designated, seems to have styl-ized a mode of communal censure for fractious couples: shrews, wife-beaters, and unfaithful spouses. Both of the mates were seated back-to-back upon a carthorse and driven through the village to the accompaniment of "rough music," a rowdy cav-alcade of neighbors whirling rattles, tinkling cowbells, and bang-ing on pots and pans. Later offenders would be impersonated or represented by effigies. William Hogarth has illustrated the sight in a fold-out engraving, as it was encountered by Samuel Butler's anti-hero Hudibras:

> Quoth he, "In all my life till now
> I ne'er saw so profane a show;
> It is a paganish invention,
> Which heathen writers often mention."

At all events, it seems less severe than being tarred and feathered, ridden out of town on a rail, or ritually castigated as Falstaff was by the merry wives of Windsor. But one does not have to be an offender in order to become the butt of a hazing. Wedding pro-cessions at Rome, attended by servants who threw out nuts to the populace, were moreover accompanied by guests who chanted scurrilous verses (*versus fescennini*), taking the bride and groom and others present—so to speak—for a ride, presumably to fend off evil omens. There was a parallel usage in the American Southwest: kidnapping a newly married couple and serenading them with kitchenware and bawdy jokes. This has been re-produced on stage and screen in the musical comedy *Oklahoma!* The play from which it was adapted, *Green Grow the Lilacs* by Lynn Riggs, had the advantage of deriving its music from genu-ine folksong, rather than from the souped-up Broadway lyricism of Richard Rodgers and Oscar Hammerstein.

The colloquial term for this rite, *shivaree*, is a contracted echo of the French *charivari*, which had become a byword for lam-pooning of all kinds. Indeed it furnished a title for the satirical magazine that featured the brilliant and unspeakably pungent cartoons of Honoré Daumier. Its opposite number in England, founded not long afterward, bore a frankly imitative subtitle: *The London Charivari*. Its tutelary persona, the nutcracker-faced Pulcinella, born at Naples, had acted in the Commedia dell' Arte, then migrated to France as Polichinelle and acquired a hump on his back, and finally rounded out his identity as that implacable puppet thoroughly anglicized, Mr. Punch. Hence the eponym for the comic weekly, *Punch, or The London Charivari*. Richard Doyle's depiction of him on the cover, which was regularly reprinted throughout the Victorian period, ironically inserted a phallic hint which harks back to Aristophanic fundamentals. Caricature, of course, is visual satire, and satire is too purposeful for sheer play. The attitude it summons up is ridicule, and to deride is to look down. In derision, we laugh at what we perceive to be ridiculous. We play with what we perceive to be ludicrous—"for recreation sake," in Falstaff's words to Prince Hal. Falstaff, both witty and the cause of wit, is the playboy *par excellence*. At the other extreme, Malvolio is Shakespeare's personification of the spoilsport, the personage who is never amused and who looks askance at the amusements of others.

The playboy is the one who goes off duty, on furlough as it were from the proprieties, like Oscar Wilde's two men-about-London who frolic in the country under the paradoxical incognito of *Ernest*; or like J. M. Synge's young Irish lout who somehow stumbles, by an accidental gesture of parricide, into having himself proclaimed *The Playboy of the Western World*; or again like Johann Strauss's debonaire philanderer, whose night on the town of Vienna is titled *Die Fledermaus*—which comes aptly close to our old-fashioned colloquialism for a round of dissipation, a *bat*. But any number can play. All the bystanders get caught up in such private holidays: diurnally as in *Le Mariage de Figaro, ou La Folle journée*, nocturnally as with the Marx Brothers in *A Night at the Opera*. Play can have both an intransitive and a transitive purport. Children go out to play, or else play a game. Prodigals can play around, or can play a trick upon somebody else. Thus we arrive at a cast of characters: the player and the one that is played upon, the trickster and he who gets tricked, the cheater and the cheated. Already we discern the outline of a comic plot. For what is a plot if not a prank, a series of tricks or transactions in trickery eliciting counterplots, whether they be tragically conspiratorial or comically intriguing? Art presupposes arrangement; even the plotlessness of absurdity has to be plotted for theatrical purposes; Samuel Beckett and Eugène Ionesco must have a full awareness of the conventions they subvert.

When Orlando rehearses his courtship in *As You Like It*, vicarious to him but not to the rest of us, Rosalind—in her masculine disguise—invites him: "Come, woo me, woo me; for now I am in a holiday humor and like enough to consent." Such a holiday humor may be considered the essence of Shakespearean comedy. Lovers are forever wooing and pairing off; and, as Don Armado pompously writes, in proposing to Jacquenetta, "The catastrophe is a nuptial." (He employs *catastrophe* in its literal sense of bringing about the final event, though the final event of *Love's Labor's Lost* will shock us by postponing the other nuptials.) Shakespeare is fond of observing holidays, rustic in the sheep-shearing festival of *The Winter's Tale* or the harvest rites of *The Tempest*, military in Henry V's oration on Saint Crispin's Day. Holidays supply titles, as well as atmosphere, for *A Midsummer Night's Dream* and *Twelfth Night*. The twelve days from Christmas to the Feast of the Epiphany constituted the season when Shakespeare's company played at court. Perdita, as a flower maiden, feels like those who play their parts in "Whitsun pastorals" or May-games. Sixteen years before, in *The Winter's Tale*, her suspicious father had told her brother:

> Go play, boy, play. Thy mother plays, and I
> Play too, but so disgrac'd a part, whose issue
> Will hiss me to my grave . . .

But, as it transpires, Leontes was not really playing the cuckold; his queen Hermione was not playing him false; and their little son Mamillius, far from playing, would soon be dying. Shakespeare's men and women and children cannot always be merely players.

His repertory is richly embellished with song and dance and pageant-like interludes ranging from spectacle to burlesque, not to mention the Erasmian interventions of the Fool. *The Two Noble Kinsmen* has a scene, which may have been composed by John Fletcher, in which the villagers entertain the Duke with a morris dance. *As You Like It* dramatizes an actual wrestling match. Many other sports, above all hunting, in pursuit of divers birds and beasts, continually figure both in the action and in the imagery. Duels tend to be dangerous recreations; but they can be sublimated into tournaments; and the pedantries of the duellists' code could be mocked by the nimble-witted Touchstone and the ill-fated Mercutio. When a lady-in-waiting seeks distraction for the weeping queen of Richard II, she proposes bowling. But neither that nor any of her other proposals—dancing, singing, and telling tales—can distract the Queen from her husband's griefs, which are soon brought home by the Gardener's allegory. The Queen's initial response has been:

> T'will make me think the world is full of rubs,
> And that my fortune runs against the bias.

The suggested entertainment modulates into tragic metaphors. If the world is a game of bowls, it is full of impediments (*rubs*), and she will suffer from its tendency to deviate in its course (*bias*). The identical terms are employed when Hamlet hesitates over "There's the rub" and Polonius undertakes to proceed by "assays of bias." Tennis animates some happy tropes for comic repartee, as when the Princess in *Love's Labor's Lost* compliments two of her ladies: "Well bandied both, a set of wit well played." It symbolizes an international insult, when the Dolphin pays the French tribute to Henry V in tennis balls. But Henry is adroit at responding in kind:

> When we have match'd our rackets to these balls,
> We will in France, by God's grace, play a set
> Shall strike his father's crown into the hazard.

Given Henry's frivolous reputation, the Dolphin has underestimated the English preparations, likening them to "a Whitsun morris dance." And the Chorus tells us how, on the eve of Agincourt, gambling among themselves over their enemies,

> The confident and overlusty French
> Do the low-rated English play at dice.

War, we may well believe, is a terrible gamble no less than it is a cruel sport. Richard III, playing for the highest stakes, can gamely face the fatal mishap of losing his horse on the battlefield: "I have set my life upon a cast, / And I will stand the hazard of the die." Other table games, such as those involving cards, can profit more than dice from the exercise of craft on the part of the players. When an earlier Dolphin (Dauphin) in *King John* hears the cry "*Vive le roi*," he assumes that his hand has been dealt a king.

> Have I not here the best cards of the game,
> To win the easy match play'd for a crown?
> And shall I now give o'er the yielded set?

Why should he surrender after so victorious an inning? *Crown* sets an ambiguous value upon what has been staked; it can mean either a kingship or a coin; and this play is notable, among the histories, for the ambiguity of its issues. *Antony and Cleopatra* contains so many locutions borrowed from card games that my late colleague, Alfred Harbage, was able to weave them into an ingenious parody of overingenious Shakespearean criticism. Shakespeare's culminating utilization of the game-within-the-game is activated by a fifth-act stage direction in *The Tempest*, instructing Prospero to pull back a curtain and discover "FERDINAND *and* MIRANDA *playing at chess*." The name of the game is not spoken in the dialogue and some contemporaries made much more use of chess, in particular Thomas Middleton, whose preoccupation with it has been reflected in T. S. Eliot's

Waste Land. None of these transpositions should really surprise us, since we have the same habits in modern speech: figurative applications of sporting phrases like *carry the ball* and *get to first base,* and of card-playing words like *bid* and *trump* and *meld* and *joker.* Nor are modern playwrights at all reluctant to exploit the dramatic effects of game-playing: witness Harold Pinter's *Birthday Party* or Edward Albee's *Who's Afraid of Virginia Woolf?*

One effect of comedy is the reduction of mature behavior to childishness. This carries with it the virtue of its defects, namely rejuvenation, such as that which the old man Demos underwent at the end of *The Clouds.* Love is the usual catalytic agent, as observed by Berowne in *Love's Labor's Lost:*

> O me, with what strict patience have I sat,
> To see a king transformed to a gnat!
> To see great Hercules whipping a gig,
> And profound Salomon to tune a jig,
> And Nestor play at push-pin with the boys,
> And critic Timon laugh at idle toys!

A mighty king has diminished himself to the size of a tiny insect. The others—prototypes of strength, wisdom, age, and critical faculties—have relapsed into the romps of childhood (with Hercules spinning a top). Berowne, who proves to be vulnerable himself, has been spying upon his companions from a hiding-place in the trees: "'All hid, all hid,' an old infant play." In his antic disposition, Hamlet too is not above playing hide-and-seek, running away from his interrogators while shouting: "Hide, fox, and all after!" In the Closet Scene he reproaches his insensitive mother for having groped her way through blind-man's buff: "What devil was't / That thus hath cozen'd you at hoodman-blind?" Tragedy is intensified in Shakespeare by unseasonable comic moments, and nowhere more poignantly than in *King Lear.* Lear, having been taught the lessons of equality by the wind and the rain and the insight of madness, reverts to an infantile shell-game: "handy-dandy, which is the justice, which is the thief?" His remembrance of his pelican daughters prompts the ragged Edgar to a crazy echo, in the manner of a nursery rhyme: "Pillicock sat on Pillicock Hill." And the bittersweet Fool presages the peek-a-boo of his master's fate in one of his topsy-turvy lyrics:

> Then they for sudden joy did weep,
>   And I for sorrow sung,
> That such a king should play bo-peep,
>   And go the fools among.

We should not be too surprised, then, when the romantic couples of comedy are treated as Jacks and Jills in *Love's Labor's Lost* and *A Midsummer Night's Dream*, or when both the choice of caskets in *The Merchant of Venice* and the mock-death of the King in *The Tempest* are counterpointed by pussycat's refrain from Mother Goose: "Ding, dong, bell, / Pussy's in the well." So the bell tolls for the drowning Alonso:

> Sea-nymphs hourly ring his knell . . .
> Hark now I hear them—Ding-dong bell.

And the tintinnabulation in the background, when Bassanio courts Portia, is a dirge for love and imagination:

> Let us all ring fancy's knell.
> I'll begin it. Ding, dong, bell.

But fancy—like the King, and even more like Saint George—cannot be kept down. It will rearise to astonish and involve and amuse us again.

B

NOTES
ON CITY
COMEDY

City comedy has never been accorded more than a very limited recognition as a genre, or rather—to employ the more precise, if hybrid, term adopted by Alastair Fowler in *Kinds of Literature*— a subgenre. Given the long and consistent association of the generic with the thematic in this mode of expression—that is to say, of comedies with cities—the compounded epithet might seem slightly redundant. My present concern is less to see it recognized amidst the terminology of criticism than to consider some aspects of the relationship it brings out. The usage seems uniquely, if not peculiarly, English, though it is not lacking in approximate counterparts elsewhere. Such adjectives as *bourgeois* or *bürgerlich* carry more of a social connotation than our awkward substantive, whereas the imported cognate *burgher* might sound too much like a comic opera. Our concept has been most pertinently invoked within the context of Elizabethan drama, where the continuous permutation of organic forms lends itself to a Polonian multiplication of formal categories, and where the redolence of local color needs to be sharply distinguished from the atmosphere of what Ben Jonson termed "some fustian country." The distinction applies with fullest force to the voluminous and heterogeneous work of Thomas Middleton, where it also serves as a rough dividing line between that playwright's comedies and his tragedies. This would seem to accord with broader distinctions between the two major dramatic genres: tragic grandeur may be more appropriately viewed from a scenic distance, comic trickery may be more readily understood in a familiar atmosphere.

Drama—*pace* Calvin and Rousseau—has usually ranked high among the attractions of urban life. The first of Thomas Heywood's arguments on its behalf was that it constituted "an ornament to the City . . ." His proud depiction of theatrical London could be paralleled by the Venetian painter, Gabriele Bella, whose view of the Piazzetta San Marco is crowded with strangers from all nations, flocking to watch the rival troupes of mountebanks perform. Epochs in the history of drama have been marked by cultural capitals: Sophocles' Athens, Shakespeare's London, Lope de Vega's Madrid. Courts, both royal and ducal, have also functioned as dramatic matrices; but, as Erich Auerbach has convincingly shown, the ideal public for Molière and the French classics was drawn conjointly from *"la cour et la ville,"* from the courtiers of Versailles and the *grande bourgeoisie* of Paris. To be sure, no city has ever been more closely, or more seminally, identified with the development of the theater than Athens. Old Comedy, while it lasted, was one of its leading institutions; the civic scene itself in war and peace, in morals and politics, in tragedy and philosophy, was the major theme of Aristophanes' invectives and celebrations. These, however, were traced back by the Athenians to a rural origin. Scholars are no longer disposed to credit, as Aristotle evidently did (*Poetics*, III), the Doric claim that comedy—both the word and the activity—originated in *kōmē*, "a village." It seems to have been derived more directly from *kōmos*, "revelry," which is etymologically related (originally signifying "village festival"), and is reenacted in a culminating episode of the play itself.

The conflated meaning, though Aristotle had cautioned against it, has exerted an influence over the critical tradition. Hence *comoedia* was defined in 1500, by the glossary of Wynkyn de Worde, as "a town song." Town, of course, interposes a further ambiguity: if it appeared to be countrified from the viewpoint of a walled and fortified city, it could look relatively citified when viewed from the open countryside. The comic stage, from its metropolitan standpoint, has habitually tended to ridicule the denizens of the small town; the zanies of the Commedia dell' Arte started as provincials from Bergamo; and communities along the Hudson River, with funny names like Hoboken or Yonkers, gain easy laughs for Broadway comedians. Town and country were brought into confrontation with one another in a theory sketched by some of the late Greek scholiasts. It was their assumption that peasants from the outlying hamlets of Attica, having been mistreated by certain townsmen, disguised themselves and repaired to Athens at night; there, in streets before the dwellings of their oppressors, they staged vocal demonstrations of protest; and, gradually evolving in an Aristophanic direction, that practice was turned over to municipal choruses, which aired common grievances and denounced aberrant citizens. This speculation gets echoed in the poetics of Antonio Minturno and other Renaissance theorists, but it had little in the way of classical substantiation. Whatever the genesis of comedy—and we have not progressed much beyond conjecture—its regular audiences would be composed of city-dwellers, who expected it to mirror the circumstances of their lives.

It has been repeatedly and perfunctorily described in the Aristotelian terms of a polar opposition to tragedy: the style colloquial rather than heroic, the characterization vulgar rather than noble, the plot fictitious rather than legendary, the ending happy rather than sorrow-laden. The lapidary description attributed to Cicero—*"imitatio vitae, speculum consuetudinis, imago ver-*

itatis"—has been handed down to us through the Latin commentators. The first and last phrases of that tripartite formula simply reaffirm the notion of *mímesis*, and might do almost as well for tragedy. It is the middle phrase, the trope of the mirror, that signalizes the difference: what is to be reflected here is custom, typical behavior, quotidian existence. Medieval tragedies could also be envisaged as metaphorical mirrors for kings or magistrates, insofar as their storied protagonists serve as awful examples illustrating cautionary object-lessons. Similarly Robert Greene and Thomas Lodge, through the choric voice of the prophet Jonah, could warn their compatriots against the fate of Nineveh in A *Looking-Glass for London and England*. Jonson's experiments in "comical satire" would add the metaphor of a scourge to that of the looking-glass, when his spokesman Asper fulminated:

> Well, I will scourge those apes;
> And to these courteous eyes oppose a mirror,
> As large as is the stage whereon we act:
> Where they shall see the time's deformity
> Anatomiz'd in every nerve and sinew,
> With constant courage and contempt of fear.

Anatomizing is still another metaphor (vivisection), anticipated by the threat "to strip the ragged follies of the time." And when the angry man goes on to speak of "pills to purge," the medical catharsis is proposed as a satirical corrective. But Jonson protested too much when he cracked the whip of a moral activist and social reformer, probably to counter the mounting Puritan charges of histrionic immorality. He would be more successful when he gave up his didactic asperity for a good-natured realism, enjoying the reflection for its own sake, and contenting himself with what naturalistic playwrights would call *"une tranche de vie."*

Old Comedy faced the reality of public situations, often so grossly caricatured and so heavily propagandized that it finally lost its satiric license. Consequently New Comedy focussed attention on private lives, shifting its milieu from the forensic center to the domestic suburbs, shying away from recognizable individuals and building up its roster of stock types. Its agons were not political contests but struggles of will between the generations, the sexes, and the classes (masters versus servants). Its titles, like its nomenclature, were inclined to set forth psychological traits: *Dyskolos* (*The Curmudgeon*), *Heauton Timorumenos* (*The Self-Tormentor*), *Le Misanthrope*, or—more cheerfully—*The Good-Natured Man*. Where tragedies are ordinarily titled after their main characters, comedies more frequently use place-names: *Romeo and Juliet*, not *The Lovers of Verona*; not *Valentine and Proteus*, but *The Two Gentlemen of Verona*. In the Latin adaptations, our principal corpus for New Comedy, the location is always significant. Plautus and Terence both concentrated on *fabulae palliatae*, plays in Greek dress rather than Roman (*togatae*). Most of these were located in a conventional Athens. Some of them took place in Hellenistic seaports, which could fitly provide accommodation for merchants, shipwrecked lovers, and long-lost recognition scenes. It was assumed, by convention, that the stage exits led at one side to the harbor and at the other to the forum. Thus the prologue to the *Menaechmi* apologetically tells us that the argument will be more or less Greekish, not truly Attic but more likely Sicilian: ". . . . *hoc argumentum graecissat, tamen / non atticissat verum sicilicissitat*."

But the actual locale, to which we are so circumstantially introduced, proves to be on the Illyrian seacoast:

> *Haec urbs Epidamnus est, dum haec agitur fabula;*
> *quando alia agetur, aliet fiet oppidum.*
> *sicut familiae quoque solent mutarier:*
> *Modo hic habitat leno, modo adulescens, modo senex,*
> *pauper, mendicus, rex, parasitus, hariolus.*

Epidamnus is where the damage will be incurred, to anticipate a subsequent pun on *damnum*, and we are likewise informed about the Syracusian prehistory, since what we shall witness, after all, is a tale of two cities, and the twins are Sicilians from Syracuse. Plautus makes it clear that, on due occasion, the stage can be whatever town the stage-directions call for. This adjustability is compared with families who move from one house to another or, to be more specific, with their transient inhabitants—though a more exact analogy would be with changeable residences, not with changing residents. Nor does the concluding list announce the cast of characters, even though the play will involve a parasite, an old man, not one but two young men, a doctor if not a soothsayer, and a prostitute if not a procurer. The juxtaposition of a beggar and a king—no comic figure (Plautus apologizes for letting his incognito Jupiter stray into the *Amphitryon*)—seems to imply a cross-section of society as a whole, rather than the standard dramatis personae. Performing a similar task some 1,500 years afterward, Machiavelli's prologue to his *Mandragola* (first published in 1524) would jocosely allude to such shifts from one locality to another. Today the scene will be Florence, the Florentine audience is told, in the manner of an officious guide pointing out the well-known landmarks. And yet again tomorrow it could be Rome or Pisa, and that might prompt us to jawbreaking laughter, for better or for worse.

> *Vedete l'apparato,*
> *Quale or vi si dimostra:*
> *Questa è Firenze vostra,*
> *Un'altra volta sarà Roma, o Pisa;*
> *Cosa da smascellarsi per le risa.*

New Comedy had been able to retain its Grecian *pallium* when it was translated to ancient Rome. When it was revived in the sixteenth century under princely patronage, it was transposed to the Tuscan vernacular and localized into the townscapes of the Italian Renaissance. The lavish revivals of Plautus in the great courtyard of the Duke's palace at Ferrara, beginning with the *Menaechmi* in 1486, prepared the way for the *commedia erudita*. Ludovico Ariosto may have been present at that performance; he seems indeed to have acted in another production of the same play seven years later. By the time his own first comedy was produced there in 1508, the Estensi rulers had built a pioneering theater, where perspective scenery could be tried out, with Mantegna among the contributing painters. But that preliminary endeavor, the *Cassaria*, happened to be set in Mytilene (Taranto), far away and long ago. During the following year it was the première of Ariosto's *Suppositi* that really inaugurated a new trend by updating the action and transferring it to where else but Ferrara? There was even a pun upon *"fè rara* [rare faith]." The play, in its initial prose version, would be restaged ten years later before Pope Leo X at the Vatican, where the scene-designer was Raphael. Yet we may wonder whether this kind of comedy would ever have been so fully reanimated, if it had not been relocated in—and fostered by—a special community. The *mise-en-scène*, both original and papal, had attempted to recreate the Ferrarese topography; and, as dramatic spectacles augmented among the rival city-states, they vied with one another in festive reconstructions of themselves.

Artists and artisans joined their skills in putting together the varied architectural vistas within a framing proscenium. The mystery plays had utilized multiple settings, where the actors moved on from *domus* to *domus*; now, by the art of perspective, many mansions could be organized into a single illusionistic prospect. This could consist of "house fronts, squares, porticoes, streets embellished with arches, columns, statues of various kinds—" according to the Mantuan impresario, Leone di Somi, "the models being taken from this city or that, ancient or modern, according to the demands of the script." Such monumental appurtenances could hardly be duplicated on the makeshift platforms of strolling players. Yet we should take a second look, among Callot's engravings of the Italian comedians, at the absorbing triptych *Les Trois Pantalons*; for, while each of these three figures—the Pantalone in person, the Capitano, and the Zanni—looms large over an unlocalized foreground, he is reduced to miniature in the background and presented onstage with other actors; and there the wings jut out to form a street scene framed by receding lines of houses on both sides. Browsing through the repertory of the Commedia dell' Arte, in the standard collection of Flamineo Scala, we may note how the setting passes on from town to town: Rome, Venice, Naples, Milan, Bologna, Florence, Mantua, and Parma. Only the final ten of these fifty scenarios are set in exotic places like Fez, Egypt, Persia, Sparta, and Arcadia; and it is significantly uncharacteristic that, instead of being comedies like the rest, they are classified as operas, excepting one tragedy and one pastoral.

Summing the matter up in Aristotelian language, Francesco Robortello flatly affirmed: ". . . no comedy can be recited if the Music and Spectacle are not employed so that the play on the stage appears to be enacted in city or town." The outdoor theater of the Romans had been constructed around a permanent *frons scaenae*, an imposing structure three stories high, symmetrically adorned with pedestals, pilasters, niches, and other components of classical architecture. Along with the entrances *"a foro"* on stage left and *"a peregre"* on stage right, five doors punctuated this ornate façade, in the composite plan of Vitruvius. The central door was understood as belonging to a royal palace in tragedy, where the two adjacent ones were assigned to strangers and sojourners. In comedy the whole array might conventionally be regarded as a row of habitations fronting on a square. But the two outermost doorways were arranged to present at least a stylized suggestion of painted scenery, with revolving panels or *periaktoi* to designate which of the three official genres held sway at the moment. The tragic décor (*"ornatus"*) would feature pillars, pediments, statues, and other royal things (*"reliquisque regalibus rebus"*). A comic panel would offer a reproduction of familiar buildings (*"imitatione communium aedificiorum"*) with windows and balconies. And since the ancients had realized from the outset that all of human experience could not be subsumed within the tragic/comic dichotomy, they left room for a *tertium quid*: a glimpse of trees, rocks, mountains, and other rustic features (*"reliquisque agrestibus rebus"*) of the satyric landscape.

Vitruvian principle could be put into practice much more flexibly and realistically through the two new technical devices of the Cinquecento, perspective painting and movable scenery. Scene design was formulated and illustrated and widely influenced by the architectural treatises of Sebastiano Serlio, which showed how raked stages, canvas side-wings, and *trompe-l'oeil* backcloths could approach the graphic effects of contemporary painting. The houses in the Comic Scene should be those of *"personaggi privati, come saria di cittadini, avocati, mercanti, parasiti, & altre simili persone."* The implication—that lawyers, merchants, and other citizens are much like professional parasites—is virtually Machiavellian. But above all (*"Ma supra il tutto"*) a bawdy-house is specified (and part of the word *Ruffiana* can be seen, in the illustration, next to the door of the smallest and nearest house), together with a church, an inn, and evidently shops. Further specifications indicate practical windows and balconies, thereby facilitating many an amorous dialogue. The contrasting Tragic Scene is graced by the statelier homes of *"grandi personaggi,"* since the high adventures and cruel deaths in ancient and modern tragedies always occur on the premises of *"Signori, Duchi, ò gran Prencipi, anzi de Rè."* As for the Satyric Scene, here Serlio follows Vitruvius in recommending trees, grass, flowers, rocks, hills, mountains, and fountains, and for good measure includes a rustic hut to house indigenous shepherds or fishermen. He goes somewhat further by accepting, and attempting to rationalize, the old confusion between *satyr* and *satire*.

Assuming that the satyr-plays were vehicles for reproof and castigation, he argues that such chidings of misbehavior could be most appropriately voiced by the *"gente rustica,"* inasmuch as rude countrymen are no respecters of persons. But this bears more resemblance to Old Comedy than to what we know about Greek satyr-drama, a form more firmly linked with tragedy, to which it served as a sportive mythological afterpiece. Serlio's bosky instructions would have their real impact upon the scenography of the pastoral. Previously it would have been much easier to devise a stage-picture involving structures rather than land-scapes. But panoramic views of nature, serried in gardens or untamed in forests, were better suited to courtly spectacles than to dramatic performances. The masque was, in some ways, an in-door version of the *fête champêtre*. It was unusual for Inigo Jones, brilliant architect though he was, to depict "a street scene in perspective of fair building," rather than plazas or groves. When he came to do so, for the antimasque of puppets and pantaloons in Jonson's *Vision of Delight*, he combined suggestions he had bor-rowed from Serlio's Tragic and Comic Scenes; and for a later masque by the Sieur de Racan, *Artenice*, he drew—with a blend-ing eclecticism—upon the Satyric Scene as well as the other two. Proscenium staging could adapt itself handsomely to interiors, when they were palatial in scale and ornamentation, like the marbled halls and angled apartments of the Bibienas, most suit-able for tragedy or opera. New Comedy has frequented exter-iors conceived as neighboring domiciles, with much business in doorways and much speculation about what might be going on inside.

The circumstance that finds lovers, enemies, or unacquainted relatives living next door to each other may be one of those coincidences that turn the sphere of comedy into such a small world after all. Accordingly, the heroine of the *Miles Gloriosus* can conceal herself by sneaking into the adjacent house and pretending to be her own twin sister, while the game of cuckoldry can rotate through three adjoining households in the scenario of *I tre becchi*. When the comic action went indoors, it was look-ing—so to speak—behind the scenes. The neo-classical play-house, shaped by aristocratic patronage, would be awkwardly and belatedly adjusted to more democratic needs and means. Its pro-portions had become too cavernous, its tormentors and traverses and flats too unrealistic, to be comfortably domesticated. Come-dy of manners was urbane, if no longer altogether urban. In making up its mind, or regulating its conduct, the English Resto-ration still deferred to whatever it meant by "the town"—an area consisting largely of lodging and coffee-houses and parks convenient for rendezvous. The privacy of the box set grew more and more confining as the middle class, succeeding the gentry, in its turn was challenged by the working class, and as the drawing-rooms of Somserset Maugham and Noel Coward were super-seded by the kitchen-sinks of John Osborne and Arnold Wesker. Yet comedy has never completely relaxed its oppidan ties.

> Patched canvas drops of American street scenes hang in almost every vaudeville and burlesque house in the country. They usu-ally depict a perspective view of a spotless street broken by car tracks, but unworn by traffic. On one side a fire plug, on the other a piece of high park wall showing signboards and paid ads of some of the town's most enterprising firms; a few hybrid flowers; above the wall green trees; overhead, a cerulean sky with summer clouds . . . From Tacoma all the way to Tallahassee, they look alike.

Several generations of comedy-teams had cracked their jokes on the "scene-in-one" (the forestage), in front of those drop curtains which the late Donald Oenslager so nostalgically recollected. And, even while he was writing, he could have pointed to recent and painstaking reproductions of New York City in its theaters: Elmer Rice's *Street Scene* (1929), where a squalid apartment-house teemed with ethnic antagonisms, or Sidney Kingsley's *Dead End* (1935), where dripping street urchins emerged from an orchestra-pit simulating the East River. Comedy was over-shadowed by melodrama in both locations.

Yet comedy—ever since the Renaissance, and preeminently with Shakespeare—has capered increasingly on playgrounds nearer to nature. The satyr-play had prefigured, as it turned out, not so much the satirical as the pastoral drama: *favola boscareccia*, for which the primary example was Torquato Tasso's *Aminta*. The over-elaborated imitation by Giambattista Guarini, *Il Pastor Fido*, which would be so widely imitated, was charac-terized as *tragicommedia boscareccia*. One of the polemical ob-jections, in the controversy it met, was that city-dwelling play-goers would have little to learn from the mouths of simple-minded rustics—not a very serious argument against the conven-

tions of Virgil and Theocritus. Precept and example for tragicomedy were relayed explicitly to England through John
Fletcher's *Faithful Shepherdess*; closer to the vein of the court
masque, it could claim no popular success. The romantic comedies of George Peele and Robert Greene, heralded at a more
exclusive level by John Lyly, brought some *al fresco* touches into
the public theater. But it was Shakespeare who imposed the
pattern that would be summed up in the stage-direction of his
editors, "*Another part of the wood* [or *forest*]," and suggestively
explained by the paradigm of Northrop Frye: the restorative conception of a "green world." The working-day world to which
Shakespeare's characters are restored, after retreat and renewal in
a wood near Athens, the Forest of Arden, or an enchanted island,
is a ducal court. But in *The Merchant of Venice*, where the place
of refuge is a country villa, the arena of conflict remains a comic
metropolis, the bustling native city of Pantaloon himself.

Treading the Plautine maze in *The Comedy of Errors*, Shakespeare still managed to stay within the purlieus of a Greco-
Roman seaport, though he meaningfully substituted a mysterious
Ephesus for a picaresque Epidamnus. His broadest and darkest
depiction of a city is the scandal-ridden Vienna of *Measure for
Measure*, whose eavesdropping Duke admits, with a shamefaced
pun: ". . . I have seen corruption boil and bubble / Till it o'er-
run the stew." That the man of Stratford could be totally at home
in London, holding his own on the chosen ground of Jonson and
Middleton, is demonstrated by the convivial humors of East-
cheap in both parts of *Henry IV*. Yet, when Falstaff was suddenly
lifted out of history to be anticlimactically set down in comedy,
he found himself rusticated to Windsor (apparently for ceremonial reasons). "Under the greenwood tree" was the characteristic site for Shakespearean comedy; and, if the stage-manager
could contribute no more than a property-hedge to its literal
flowering, then the resources of speech and song were ready to
supply—as John Keats would observe—an impression of ver-
dure. At the other extreme the Jonsonian ambience, whether at
Saint Paul's Walk or Saint Mark's Square, was invariably and

traditionally urbanized. Englishmen, in their lifestyle and out-look, have been prone to oscillate between country and city. Shakespeare and Jonson, in their respective venues, seem to confirm an inherent disparity between the romantic and the satirical modes of comedy. But *romantic* is never a satisfactory label, least of all for a dramatic vehicle; C. L. Barber's *festive* might catch the merry note more aptly, or even Mikhail Bakhtin's *carnivalesque*.

The important matter, at all events, is the divergence between these two distinctive strains. M. C. Bradbrook recognizes this in *The Structure of Elizabethan Comedy*, where—taking a hint from Lear's Fool—she subdivides her material into "sweet" and "bitter." The so-called bitter strain, it should be added, is the one that stretches back to the mainstream of New Comedy, whereas sweet comedy seems to have been something of a novelty with— and a specialty of—the Elizabethans. Antithetical parallels could be multiplied: wit and humor, derision or risibility, put-down versus up-beat. Comparably, in earlier Italian literature Francesco De Sanctis discerned the interplay of two opposing impulses: idyll (*"ozio di villa"*) and carnival (*"ozio di città"*). The latter, in a different sense from Bakhtin's, was related to the *canti carnascialeschi*, the licensed buffoonery of the towns. The former connoted the secluded elegance of the villas; it fostered idealization, as opposed to caricature. Antithesis is converted to paradox in an overstated essay by Vernon Lee, "The Italy of the Elizabethan Dramatists." If, despite "the monstrous immorality of the Italian Renaissance," its writers could escape into an innocent pastoralism, she speculated, then it was left for dramatists like John Webster and Cyril Tourneur to recreate those sins and vices in England's "purer moral atmosphere." Italy was unquestionably ill-famed as a breeding-ground of poison, plot, popery, and Machiavellianism, especially corrupting for susceptible English travellers: *"Inglese italianato è diavolo incarnato."* But, more than any other land, it also provided a wholesome playground for Shakespearean comedy.

And Italy cannot be said to have exercised any monopoly over sinister motivation; France, to seek no farther, is the country of

The Massacre at Paris, Bussy d'Ambois, and *The Atheist's Trag-edy.* Nor was English life deficient in criminal deeds, so far as that goes, such as the case-history dramatized in *Arden of Fever-sham* and apocryphally fathered on Shakespeare. Sordid crimes befalling commoners might have been considered unworthy of dramatization by classical-minded critics. Some degree of hesita-tion is registered by the Induction to *A Warning for Fair Women,* where the tutelary spirit of Tragedy—after contending with per-sonifications of History and Comedy for control of the stage—apologizes to the audience:

> My scene is London, native and your own;
> I sigh to think my subject too well known. . . .

Her subject is the stuff of sensational broadsheet journalism rather than of grandiose historical chronicles. Take away the sensation of violence, leaving adultery and death, as Thomas Heywood did in *A Woman Killed with Kindness,* and you have a preview of domestic drama, its ethical departures emphasized by the paradoxical title and embodied in the personage of the sym-pathetic cuckold. Heywood strove to bring the middle class into the realm of chronicle history in *The Life and Death of Sir Thomas Gresham, with the Building of the Royal Exchange.* Most of these documentaries took an admonitory and moralistic tone, which recalls the occasional urban echoes in the moralities and interludes. The transition is evident in a hybrid play like *The Three Ladies of London* (1581) and its sequel, where the abstrac-tions are secularized with cockney overtones. Jonson was to re-fine upon this process, but not wholly to transcend it, with *The Devil is an Ass.* In the pseudo-Shakespearean morality, *The Lon-don Prodigal,* a harsh outline is again filled in with local color-ing. The prodigal motif repeats itself not infrequently, since the scriptural parable was reinforced by the clash between errant sons and ultimately forgiving fathers in New Comedy.

Playwrights could be vague about foreign lands, and careless about shifting scenes from one territory—or period—to another.

In the two plots of *Satiromastix*, under the stress of an altercation with Jonson, "the War of the Theaters," Marston and Thomas Dekker yoked together Augustan Rome and Norman England. Patriotism and xenophobia, which gathered full scope in the histories, animated lesser episodes like the international courtship in William Haughton's *An Englishman for my Money*. Heywood truckled to such sentiments, as he did to capitalistic enterprise, in his *Four Prentices of London, with the Conquest of Jerusalem*; his heroes had rehearsed for their crusading triumphs by selling groceries, jewelry, haberdashery, and dry-goods respectively. This attempt to wrap commerce in the trappings of romance provoked an upper-class response from Francis Beaumont's *Knight of the Burning Pestle*, which burlesques a play-within-a-play entitled *The London Merchant* and employs the anti-romantic formula of *Don Quixote* to demythologize an enchanted forest into Waltham Green. With *The Shoemaker's Holiday* (1599) Dekker had already glorified the middle-class workshop-household and established the genial trandesman as hero. Simon Eyre's success-story was authenticated by the chronicles, and had figured in Thomas Deloney's *Gentle Craft* along with two saints' legends advertising the same trade. Touchstone, the master-goldsmith of *Eastward Ho*, is such another benevolently paternalistic employer, presiding over the Hogarthian fable of an idle and an industrious apprentice, while the golden quest of the new-world adventurer, Sir Petronel Flash, winds up at the Isle of Dogs, a garbage-dump in the Thames.

Eastward Ho (1605), written in an unlikely collaboration between Jonson and Marston together with George Chapman, was a successor to *Westward Ho* and a predecessor of *Northward Ho* (both by Dekker collaborating with Webster), which dealt with unattractive triangles of citizens' wives, cuckolded merchants, and gallants-about-town. Those centrifugal titles are not as expansive as their transatlantic reverberations in modern ears; they were river-cries—if not street-cries—of London, when boatmen ferried passengers up and down and across the Thames. This seamy-sided trilogy, all three within a year or so of *Othello*,

Macbeth, and *King Lear*, bears witness to the many-levelled range of Jacobean drama. Even within the precincts of city comedy, two schools were now diverging. To the more easygoing tendency, the sentimental cult of homespun virtue, the reaction was a reversion, not less observant because it was hard-boiled, combining—in its worldly wisdom and resourceful roguery—the oldest traditions of New Comedy with the latest muck-raking exposures of the Coney-Catching Pamphlets. The protean Middleton emerged as a frequent collaborator, working early with Dekker on the breezy topicalities of *The Roaring Girl*. He proceeded to put his own stamp upon a prolific sequence of vivid and fast-moving comedies before turning, with incisive effect, to Italianate (or, in the most notable instance, *The Changeling*, Hispanic) tragedy. Under Cavalier or Restoration auspices, the attitude toward the citizenry would be scornful or patronizing; with the gradual ascendancy of the bourgeoisie, it would once more be softened and sentimentalized.

Though he is adept at portraying the colorful vagrants of the underworld, Middleton's recurrent issue is the tension between the landed gentry and the money-grubbing shopkeepers. The rise and fall of Quomodo, the social-climbing usurer of *Michaelmas Term*, lodges a serious reservation against the Touchstones and Simon Eyres. Twenty-five years after *A Trick to Catch the Old One*, Philip Massinger reworked the situation in *A New Way to Pay Old Debts* (1633), casting it into the melodramatic shadow of the mortgage-brandishing Sir Giles Overreach. During that era of sharpened commercial pressures, from Elizabeth's last years through James's reign, drama became an implicit "critique of society," which has been thoughtfully elucidated by L. C. Knights in his *Drama and Society in the Age of Jonson*. Yet, as an underlying motive, "the acquisitive attitude" has been one of the comic universals. The axiom that everything has its price carried the corollary that men and women—some or all, depending on the playwright's cynicism—are reducible to rogues and whores. If they are unwilling to engage in the general chicanery, if they are not deceitful coney-catchers, then they are credulous gulls, for Jonson at any rate. And if they are more eager to cheat than most of the others, then it is the irony of ironies to behold the cheater cheated, the knave exposed as fool. The terse concluding statement in the Plautine acrostic that summarizes *Volpone*, *"all are sold,"* has a double meaning: all are bartered, all are fooled. This could not have happened anywhere else with such guile, such seductiveness, or such bedazzlement as in Venice, the most mercantile of cities, the delusive capital of Shylock and Iago.

Jonson, the congenital Londoner, had first made his mark with *Every Man in his Humor* (1598), but it had been situated in Florence by the original text, which would be naturalized in the Folio version (1616), where "Thorello" and "Musco" became "Kitely" and "Brainworm," while "Friary" and "Rialto" became "Tower" and "Exchange." Though we cannot precisely date the metamorphosis, it may well have been Jonson's participation in *Eastward Ho* that determined him to anglicize his future work for the stage, just when he was beginning to envision remoter regions through the scenic possibilities of the masque. His first play set in London, *The Silent Woman* (1609), confined itself to the more fashionable quarters; fittingly, it was performed by child actors in one of the private theaters, and would be most highly rated by the generation of John Dryden and Samuel Pepys. His only other comedy in prose, *Bartholomew Fair* (1614), is his broadest and most atmospheric evocation of low-life in its sights and sounds and smells. At his most effective in *The Alchemist* (1610), he there repatriated and tightened up the structure and the strategy of *Volpone*. The house in Blackfriars where the coneys are gulled could have abutted on Jonson's personal residence. With the exception of one neighborly chorus gossiping outside, all of the action goes on within it, moving from room to room with the door-slamming acceleration of a Georges Feydeau. Jonson proclaims his dramaturgic homecoming in the prologue:

> Our scene is London, 'cause we would make known,
> No country's mirth is better then our own.
> No clime breeds better matter for your whore,

> Bawd, squire, impostor, many persons more,
> Whose manners, now call'd humors, feed the stage.

The idealistic endeavors of Renaissance humanism to emulate and outrival its classical precedents are turned upside down in this declaration. Its first two lines read like an ironic repetition of the couplet quoted above from A *Warning for Fair Women* (1599). Jonson's fragmentary and posthumous pastoral, *The Sad Shepherd*, would promise "a fleece / To match or those of Sicily or Greece," woven out of "such wool, / As from mere English flocks his Muse can pull." Here the mock-encomium of the last three lines is the unpatriotic boast that England can outdo all other nations, when it comes to nurturing *mauvais sujets*.

No more than four specific exemplars are mentioned: "impostor," broadly relevant to nearly every comedy; "whore" and "bawd," momentarily applicable to Doll Common and Face; and "squire," referring concretely but untypically to the minor figure of Kastril. Yet Jonson must have had, at the back of his mind, the roll-call of classical archetypes that Terence rather wearily enumerates in his prologues: *senex iratus*, *servus currens*, *parasitus edax*, *miles gloriosus*, and the rest. And Sir Philip Sidney, in defending "the right use of *Comedy*," had instanced the eye-opening display "of a niggardly *Demea*, of a crafty *Davus*, of a flattering *Gnatho*, of a vainglorious *Thraso*," all of them Terentian prototypes—Demea from the *Adelphoe*, Davus from the *Andria* or the *Phormio*, Gnatho and Thraso from the *Eunuchus*. Any repertory company, whether the Commedia dell' Arte or Hamlet's players at Elsinore, must operate through typecasting with such roles. When Shakespeare revivified the *topos* of the world as stage, *theatrum mundi*, he allotted seven parts to be successively experienced by one developing individual. Jonson's more collective outlook stressed the constants of human nature, though he seems here to have reached the point of reconciling humors with manners. Having left behind his reforming zeal to put every man out of his humor, he was all the happier in his delineation of humorous varieties and oddities, which could be sorted out and codified by the norms of classical decorum. But psychology never freed itself from typology. He would not, as a classicist, have questioned the conditions laid down by Ovid for poetic survival:

> *Dum fallax servus, durus pater, inproba lena*
> *Vivent et meretrix blanda, Menandros erit.*

Jonson went out of his way to smooth Christopher Marlowe's nervous translation of this elegiac couplet from the *Amores*:

> Whilst slaves be false, fathers hard, or bawds be whorish,
> Whilst harlots flatter, shall Menander flourish.

Immortality is uncertain, however, if it is contingent upon the persistence of unchanging models and customs. When slavery has been abolished, when parasitism is no longer acceptable as a profession, when women are released from the subordination and effacement that constrained Menander's heroines, some of the stereotypes get outmoded and the conventions need to be modified. Insofar as these advances are less than complete, New Comedy continues to revive—or, at all events, survive—in the realization that many of its *personae* are still with us, *mutatis mutandis*. "*Plus ça change, plus c'est la même chose*" is one of its stalest and most durable one-liners, true enough as far as it goes, but never very encouraging.

Introducing *Terence in English*, his Elizabethan translator wrote: "He will tell you the nature of the fraudulent flatterer, the grim and greedy old sire, the roistering ruffian, the mincing minion, and the beastly bawd, that in telling the truth by these figments, men might become wise to avoid such vices, and learn to practise virtue." Stated with such generality, this comment allows for broader applications. Yet, when the roistering Thraso and the flattering Gnatho were exhumed in the academic guise of Ralph Roister Doister and Matthew Merrygreek, they were ineptly and incompletely reincarnated. Comedy, more than tragedy, is a creature of its times. Responding to the urbanization of the Renaissance it was soon caught up in that cultural process, and commenced to lose the distance needed for maintaining a critical vantage-point. *La cour* could laugh at *la ville* when the première of *Le Bourgeois gentilhomme* took place before Louis XIV at his Château de Chambord. During the eighteenth century, satire was at its sharpest in theatrical pieces like John Gay's *Beggar's Opera* or Alain-René Lesage's *Turcaret*; but sentiment was taking over, with a newer bourgeois audience which preferred its drama to dwell upon family rather than business. It is not surprising, confronted with so wide a diversity in ideological premises, that the nineteenth century should wonder whether or not it was a time for comedy. Since by then the novel had everywhere been confirmed as the *genre par excellence* of its age, perhaps we might more positively conclude that the heritage of city comedy is best sought in the prose fiction of Balzac, Dickens, Gogol, and Joyce.

C

VEINS OF
HUMOR

Critical discussion of humor is bound to suffer from the realization that it is evoked more readily than explained, and that it has therefore been more anthologized than analyzed. Inherent in its pleasurable nature is a tendency to ward off serious treatment, to fight shy of interpretation, and consequently to defy analysis. There does exist a two-volume *History of English Humour*, published by the Reverend A. G. L'Estrange in 1877, and it is almost as desultory as *Tristram Shandy*. Qualified exponents of the subject—Harold Nicolson, J. B. Priestley, Stephen Potter—have rambled on about it pleasantly. But, in view of the unending and inconclusive effort of theorizing that has been expended on comedy, or more precisely the comic, we may well be surprised that so little of it has come to grips with the humorous. A persistent if not always consistent awareness of the expanding position that this peculiar element has occupied within the wider domain, from Ben Jonson to George Meredith, has been amply documented in *The Idea of Comedy*, a compilation of the most relevant texts from English criticism, edited with an illuminating commentary by W. K. Wimsatt, to which I am gratefully indebt-ed. Perhaps it may suggest a continuity, or facilitate an access to some of the varied problems raised by the subject, if I try to sketch a rough outline of what this keyword has meant to many of those who have conjured with it.

Some of them have shied away from definition, in the obscurantist fear lest we murder to dissect. Others, more for-tunately for our purpose, have shown a Houdini-like compulsion to disentangle the mystery they profess. One of the anti-definers, S. J. Perelman, puts us in our academic place by remarking that "Humour is purely a point of view, and only the pedants try to classify it." Perelman's vein is truly one which challenges classifi-cation, depending as it does on an inimitable style and even more upon a point of view toward the multiplicity of preexisting styles. Yet it exudes a pedantry of its own, which invites a more meticu-lous scrutiny. Some of his writing, indeed, may already be need-ing footnotes. In contrast to the ironic naiveté of earlier Ameri-can humorists, Perelman displayed a parodic *savoir faire*. In his later years, by shifting his residence to England, he attested its traditional claims as the homeland of humor, where a richer backlog of conventions and clichés would continue to offer him laughing matter. On the negative side, his gesture seemed to confirm the earlier impression of Charles Dickens that the Amer-icans are not really a humorous people; certainly there is not much Dickensian jollity in the harsh transatlantic derision of *Martin Chuzzlewit*. On the other hand, it will be remembered that Americans have cracked many jokes about the Englishman who misses the point of a joke.

The notion that humor ought somehow to be treated as an undefinable *je-ne-sais quoi* has a tradition behind it which is ballasted by the skeptical authority of Swift:

> What Humor is, not all the tribe
> Of logic-mongers can describe.

Nonetheless Swift, being neither a logic-monger nor a pedant, went so far as to link the phenomenon at hand with the larger inscrutability of life itself. Here, as contrasted with those collateral gifts of conversation, wit, and raillery,

> Here, only Nature acts her part,
> Unhelped by practice, books, or art.

This conversational gift is not only odd and grotesque; it is also wild—a natural and spontaneous growth which accordingly cannot be cultivated and would merely be spoiled by the joyless exercises of affectation.

> 'Tis never by invention got;
> Men have it when they know it not.

Henry Fielding would differ markedly in his fiction, insofar as he would view affectation as "the only source of the true Ridiculous." But when he explicitly addressed himself to the concept of humor, in *The Covent-Garden Journal*, he would emphasize the vagueness of the word and the variety of opinions about it. And yet for all the pluralism and skepticism that have beclouded its ultimate signification, one aspect of it seems to have been clearly and widely understood: whatever humor might or might not be, it was thoroughly English. Thus incidentally, in the course of his ode "The Manners," William Collins paused to tender a patriotic tribute:

> O *Humour*, thou whose name is known
> To *Britain's* favor'd isle alone . . .

Alone? Is humor, then, to be regarded as the exclusive property of the English? The name itself, which Charles Baudelaire linked pertinently with its opposite number, *spleen*, was exported to other languages as a conscious anglicism. A notable example is furnished by Luigi Pirandello's monograph *L'Umorismo*, but Pirandello himself is an eloquent witness to the fact that humor could speak other tongues. The standard English spelling, ending in -*our*, interestingly enough, has been affected by the French. American usage favors the Latin suffix -*or*—which, as it happens, was used both by Jonson, in some of his quartos, and by Dickens, in his manuscripts. Fernand Baldensperger has surveyed the semantic history of the term and registered some of the intercultural reactions. He informs us, among other matters, that Montesquieu distinguished between *l'humeur des Anglais* and the Gallic *esprit*, that Voltaire found a closer translation in *chagrin* and Lessing a German counterpart in *Laune*. Traditionally the Frenchman has looked upon the Englishman as an individual who takes his pleasures sadly—more given to morosity than gaiety, according to Madame de Staël, and hence better typified by Swiftian misanthropy than by Molièresque sociability. She concludes, without much concern for the evidence, that English literature is lacking in good comedies. An actual French witness during the Restoration, the Seigneur de Saint-Evremond, had praised English comedy for its naturalness, though later critics have been more struck by the comparative artificiality of the plays he must have seen.

The capacity for laughter is doubtless a universal quality, one of the few that differentiates human beings from beasts. But the mode whereby it manifests itself and the objects that stimulate it seem to be capable of multiform variation: national, regional, social, sexual, cultural, ethnic. Such variations have a good deal to tell us, both about the laughers and about those who are not amused, the agelasts. Although many of Britain's greatest wits have been Irishmen, Englishmen have customarily taken a condescending view of Hibernian humor, sometimes equating it with the type of *non sequitur* known as a bull. It is reported of the early Sorbonne that one of the scholastic theses disputed there was whether or not a German could have wit. Yet *Galgenhumor* is not a uniquely British commodity, and the Nonsense Rhymes of Edward Lear have something in common with the *Unsinnspoesie* of Christian Morgenstern. One of the sexes has been charged by the other with a lack of humor—despite the sparkling instance of Mistress Millamant, "a woman, and a kind of humorist." That charge, we may suspect, goes back to the days when it would have been considered unladylike to appreciate Rabelais. My old teacher, George Lyman Kittredge, was fond of maintaining that Jews, though often witty, were basically humorless. This assumption may simply have been a confession of insensibility to a wry *Weltanschauung* more widely shared today than it may have been half a century ago.

"The stroke of the great humorist is world-wide, with lights of Tragedy in his laughter," wrote Meredith in his lecture-essay *On Comedy and on the Uses of the Comic Spirit*. He was speaking contextually of Cervantes—whose quintessential Spanishness, to the contrary notwithstanding, has been underlined by many another commentator. Meredith's theories, particularly with regard to the civilizing influence of women, seem to have weathered better than most of his novels, where the Comic Spirit all too frequently seems to be laughing up her diaphanous sleeve. His impressionistic rhapsodizing tells us little about "the spirit of Humour," except to stress its rough-and-tumble heterogeneity. He is mainly concerned with a highly rarefied comedy of manners, which envisions its prototype in the lost works of Menander and discerns its masterpiece in the atypical *Misanthrope* of Molière. On most other comic writers he sounds unconvincing, since he is less interested in drawing concrete distinctions than in building up a sort of composite paradigm. Now, granted the argument of Joseph Addison that the test of true wit is translation, that genuine humor ought not to be bounded by frontiers, still there is much to be learned from the untranslatable or from a foreign perspective. Mr. Punch may embody the typically English figure of fun, yet he was born in Naples, and acquired his hump in France. It would be instructive to contrast him with his semblances in other cultures: the French Guignol, the German Kasperl, the Turkish Karaghiosis.

The particularity of English humor seems, at all events, to have been universally acknowledged. Locally it was a matter of self-recognition—and of self-congratulation, too, for John Ruskin. Some drawings in an exhibition at Oxford by one of *Punch's* most popular illustrators, John Leech, led Ruskin to speculate on "a moral and metaphysical question, to determine the share which English humor has in completing our courage and affection, in enabling us to bear hardship with a smile and convey reproof in play." So heroic a virtue is bound to have its invidious defect, since it invites a Podsnappian comparison with the lesser breeds: "I believe the total want of this faculty in the Italian mind to be at the root of much of its cruelty, and to give more dangerous languor to its vices." Ruskin himself was obviously no humorist, although the unconscious irony of such a passage is not without its humorous overtones. Broader-minded critics, like Meredith, managed to give the English humorists a cosmopolitan tinge by making honorary Englishmen out of Cervantes and even Rabelais and Aristophanes. Among Continental observers Hippolyte Taine, past master of French generalizations about England, summed up by alluding to the bitter taste of its humor. Though he was not familiar with the useful American compound *deadpan*, that was the very feature he singled out: *"la plaisanterie d'un homme qui en plaisantant garde une mine grave."*

Observation at the international level generally reflects the observer as well as the observed. If a certain nation tends to jest with staid and sober mien even to the point of melancholia, another nation may elude high seriousness by grimaces, gesticulations, and frivolous habits. Such, at any rate, has vulgarly been the English stereotype for the French. From first to last, the British Channel has offered a two-way thoroughfare for historical interaction and mutual appraisal. French Anglicists, among whom Professor Louis Cazamian held a respected place, have contributed special insights to the appreciation of English culture. They were especially fascinated by *The Development of English Humour*—to cite the title of a small book brought out by Cazamian in 1930 and much revised and augmented in 1952. Therein he does not deny the British their birthright, but he propounds his own thesis about its provenance. His starting-point is the relative paucity of humor in Anglo-Saxon literature, a circumstance which has seldom been questioned though variously explained. Thence he moves on quickly to the period of Chaucer, and to a humorous flowering which can be readily illustrated. What has happened meanwhile? The Norman Conquest, of course. Mirth has come to Merry England largely as an importation from the Continent, personified by that gifted woman of letters, Marie de France. The catalyst for English humor has been the *esprit gaulois*.

We are reinforced in the tentative conclusion that humor is not an instinctive racial trait, though there are solidly circumstantial reasons for the local habitation with which it has repeatedly been associated; and likewise that, since different races have differed in their expression of it, it had best be studied in the widest possible context. However, if we are curious why the English presented themselves to the world—in Oliver Goldsmith's phrase—as "a nation of humorists," we must further inquire why they found it necessary to supplement the more usual conception of wit with the idea of humor. The dichotomy between them has its *locus classicus* in the spirited essay "On Wit and Humour" that introduces William Hazlitt's *Lectures on the English Comic Writers* (1819). Those two terms had travelled far together since the seventeenth century, now loosely synonymous and again in polar opposition. Etymology reveals a kind of paradox, since—while *humor* comes intact from the Latin—*wit* has an Anglo-Saxon origin. Deriving from the verb *witan*, "to know," it may boast a historical kinship with *wisdom*. Its Greek equivalent was *Euphues*, a designation borrowed by John Lyly from Roger Ascham, for whom it adjectivally signified a well-trained good mind. Other Elizabethans employed it to mean imagination—or else what Samuel Taylor Coleridge might have called fancy. Its shades and shifts of meaning form the basis of a pyrotechnical sequence in Alexander Pope's *Essay on Criticism*.

A similar ambiguity is conveyed by the French *esprit*, which seems less whole-heartedly committed to spirituality than its portentous German synonym, *Geist*. The striking distinction is that, in comparison with the intellectualistic connotations of wit, the reverberations of *humor* are corporeal, not to say materialistic or earthbound. The first of nine definitions listed in Dr. Johnson's *Dictionary* is quite literally "moisture." More specifically, according to ancient and medieval physiology, this denoted the four fluids of the human body—choler (or bile), melancholy, phlegm, and blood—which in turn had been determined by the four elements. During the Renaissance a growing emphasis was placed upon the psychological consequences of these physical attributes. Ideally, it was thought, they should commingle in due proportion, originally designated as *temperament*. In practice, one of the humors usually predominated over the others, thereby determining whether the individual *disposition*—another technical term—would be choleric (or bilious), melancholic, phlegmatic, or sanguine. An ingenious Spanish physician, Juan Huarte, even published a treatise in 1575, *Examen de ingenios para les ciencias*, suggesting that all infants be examined at birth and assigned to their subsequent careers in accordance with their temperamental predispositions. That deterministic program came under the strictures of the Inquisition for its implicit challenge to the freedom of the will. But it was translated and circulated in England, where it was undoubtedly read by Ben Jonson.

More casually, humor could be conceived as a person's state of mind at the moment: a mood, a caprice, a whim, an inclination to be indulged—or humored (Shakespeare was apparently the first to use the verbal form). Persons subject to such passing states—moody, capricious, whimsical—were said to be humorous. But this is at the other extreme from a psychic condition rigidly predetermined by a predominant humor or ruling passion, a master faculty or *idée fixe*. It is the latter that animates the stock figures of the comic stage, as they have been fixed by convention and stiffened by decorum. And it was Jonson who took the critical step of transposing the category of humor from the plane of physiognomy to the sphere of comedy. Actually, his first great theatrical success, *Every Man in his Humor* (1598), was preceded one year before by George Chapman's play, *An Humorous Day's Mirth*. The catchword seems to have accorded with certain movements in the direction of satire and the fashionable humor of melancholy. With Corporal Nym it gathered a Shakespearean resonance: "And that's the humor of it." Jonson's original version of *Every Man in his Humor* was a conventionally Italianate piece of work, whose resounding title was hardly more than a quasi-proverbial phrase. It was in the programmatic Induction to *Every Man out of his Humor* (1599) that Jonson fully asserted his individuality and formally announced a new comic dispensation.

This dialogue allows his angry spokesman Asper to be drawn out by two judicious interlocutors into a psychophysical description of humor, which he thereupon brings into the playhouse:

> It may, by metaphor, apply itself
> Unto the general disposition:
> As when some one peculiar quality
> Doth so possess a man that it doth draw
> All his affects, his spirits, and his powers,
> In their confluctions, all to run one way,
> This may be truly said to be a humor.

Jonson goes on to insist, like Swift, that humor is ingrained and not to be achieved by affectation, although one can think of Jonsonian characters who come closer to Fielding's in that respect. The additional metaphors that here come into play are the standard properties of the didactic satirist: mirror, scourge, anatomy. *Every Man out of his Humor* marks the first stage of an experimental trilogy described as "comical satire." These were failures as comedies, nor did they succeed in the reforming endeavor to which they were dedicated. Asper, under the guise of Macilente, enters the drama itself, seeking to castigate and cure the distempered dramatis personae. But if men are so physically conditioned as the theory maintains, can a mere reflection of their behavior move them to change their motives? The stage would seem less suitable than the judge's bench or the psychoanalyst's couch for putting men out of their humors. Jonson evades the dilemma in his maturest plays by again permitting every man to enact his humor freely, for better or worse. We speak broadly of the genre he devised as the comedy of humors; yet his ripest characters are by no means monomaniacal; Volpone is not a hedgehog but a fox. The asperities of Asper seem to have been closely parodied by the punitive language of Jaques in *As You Like It*, whose talk about flaying and purging may be interpreted as Shakespeare's genial burlesque of the stern Jonsonian attempt to impose poetic justice upon a fallible humanity.

The melancholy Jaques is cast in that role which Hamlet, while enumerating the members of a repertory troupe, terms "the humorous man." The principal characteristic of this personage, moodiness, stems from a fundamental dissatisfaction with the world which is not unlike that of the tragic malcontent. Hamlet, who combines both parts, is deliberately—if grimly—comic when he assumes his "antic disposition." But the adjective *humorous*, for Shakespeare, indicates a potential subject for fun and not a funster. Bardolph and the other followers of Falstaff are denominated "irregular humorists" in the Folio's list of actors' names for *The Second Part of Henry IV* (that noun itself does not appear in Shakespeare's text). The title-page of the Quarto promises to include "the humours of sir Iohn Falstaffe." Note the plural: the Prince has previously labelled his companion "that trunk of humors," and John Dryden will echo the epithet in hailing him as "a miscellany of humors." Falstaff thus transcends the single-humored type by his sheer diversity and flexibility. He himself is his best interpreter when, after having somewhat unexpectedly run away with the show in Part I, he makes his self-heralding entrance into Part II: "Men of all sorts take a pride to gird at me. The brain of this foolish-compounded clay, man, is not able to invent anything that intends to laughter, more than I invent or is invented on me. I am not only witty in myself, but the cause that wit is in other men."

Falstaff has been discoursing about wit; but, as its sentient object, he stands in a strategic position to formulate its relationship with humor. For he is not only a butt, a figure of fun, a cause that wit is in other men; he is moreover witty in himself, a laughingstock who can join in the laugh and end by ironically turning it against his would-be mockers, as in the mock-epic of Gadshill. Compare him with Bardolph and observe the difference. Except for his gruff objurgations, Bardolph has no defense against jokes about his nose; Falstaff has endless *ripostes* to the gibes about his belly, and excels the others in the inventiveness of his self-mockery—an imaginative flow which, as he later soliloquizes, has its unbounded source of inspiration in sherry. Inasmuch as bellies and noses are bodily rather than mental, and natural rather than artificial, they are the stuff of humor; and once set forth, it becomes the task of wit, as Hazlitt would argue, to perceive and expose such exaggerated appurtenances. By the same token it follows that wit is impersonal, in the Coleridgean sense that it could be remarked by any observer, whereas humor—Coleridge maintains—"always more or less partakes of the character of the speaker." Where the wits are bland suitors, walking gentlemen, and men about town, whose urbane repartee is more or less interchangeable, humorous characters always have idiosyncratic voices of their own, and Falstaff plays the dual personality of the Erasmian fool who brings out the follies of other men.

Falstaff's statement about his role-playing helps to explain the central figure he is destined to cut in any consideration of English comedy. Furthermore, it has far-reaching implications which can illustrate and interrelate much of the esthetic theory that has attempted to analyze the comic. Most of the theorists have had something in their grasp, like the blind men with the elephant; what still needs to be shown is the connection between the parts. By and large, their views can be boiled down to two schools of thought. One of these, following Thomas Hobbes, emphasizes superiority; the other, with Immanual Kant, stresses incongruity. In other words, the first concentrates on the witty viewpoint, the second on the humorous situation. Among the moderns, Sigmund Freud aligns himself with the first by focussing on self-expression and personal animus (*Witz* meaning both wit and joke). What he dismisses as harmless wit can be looked on as playful humor, whose protagonist is *homo ludens*, the hero of

Johan Huizinga's brilliant treatise on play as a component of civilization. The same word, *ridicule*, was utilized by both Stendhal and Lord Kames as a touchstone for wit. The playfulness of humor is characterized by Stendhal as *le plaisant* and by Kames as risibility. These terminological variances might be reconciled by speaking normatively of the ridiculous, on the one hand, and of the ludicrous on the other. Laughter is the common denominator between *laughing at* and *laughing with*, and Falstaff is our agent in both camps.

However, prompted by Falstaffian instinct perhaps, we anticipate. Historically, the explicit antithesis between wit and humor seems to have emerged from the hard-hitting controversy between Dryden and Thomas Shadwell. Jonson's belated disciple, Shadwell was trying to revive the older comedy of humors, while Dryden inclined toward a newer, French-inspired, more elegant comedy of manners. In his preface to *An Evening's Love* (1671), disclaiming humor on his own part, he declared that Jonson had been the only playwright who practised it—probably in order to compensate for his deficiency in wit. But meanwhile humor had been acquiring a broader and more positive significance, and could not so tartly be put down. Sir William Temple paid especial attention to it in his important essay *On Poetry* (1690), wherein it is traced to Shakespeare rather than Jonson. Pointing to the essential Englishness of both the word and the vein, Temple attributes this favorable outgrowth to the native soil, the changeable climate, and above all a government which tolerates free opinion and free speech. The environment fosters an individualism which brings out eccentricities to a degree not paralleled elsewhere. Where the conformities of the Continent are expressed through the same old typical characters, England glories in its Originals, whose variety is mirrored in the theater. "We are not only more unlike one another than any nation I know, but we are more unlike ourselves too at several times."

William Congreve, though he claimed novelty for his subject, amplified a number of Temple's points in his letter to John Dennis *Concerning Humour in Comedy* (1695); the predominance of the English, their singularity as individuals, and "the great freedom, privilege, and liberty which the common people of England enjoy." Rather a wit than a humorist, as Samuel Johnson would testify, Congreve vaguely undertook to synthesize the two categories; but it was rather inconsistent of him, as the future creator of Millamant, to question women's humor. Dennis himself, an austere and blunt neo-classicist, advocated humor at the expense of wit because he felt that characters of lower rank were more appropriate to comedy. Addison expectably proposed a compromise (in *Spectator* 35) through one of his allegorical pedigrees, where Humour was the offspring of Wit and Mirth. In *Sensus Communis: An Essay on the Freedom of Wit and Humour* (1709), the Earl of Shaftesbury posed the high-minded argument that truth and justice could not be vulnerable to ridicule (yet Socrates himself had; after all, been injuriously ridiculed by Aristophanes). A social conflict between the aristocracy and the bourgeoisie was implied by George Farquhar's *Discourse on Comedy*: "The Courtier cries out for *wit* and *purity of style*; the Citizen for *humor* and *ridicule*." The ideological tension was confirmed by Goldsmith, in terms which would soon be reversed: "Wit raises human nature above its level; humor acts a contrary part, and equally depresses it."

But Goldsmith was engaged in a rear-guard action on behalf of superior wit, and so was the third edition of the *Encyclopaedia Britannica* (1788–97) when it stated that humor might not be "perfectly consistent with true politeness." Vocal laughter, which Lord Chesterfield had condemned for its democratic vulgarity, would ring loud in the nineteenth century. When Johnson was depicted by Sir John Hawkins as "the most humorous man I ever saw," and likened to the old comedians, the reference was not to his fits of depression but to his bouts of jocularity. To be sure, he offered a fine illustration for Temple's and Congreve's point that English culture fostered originality of character. Further illustrations are abundant in such books as Edith Sitwell's *English Eccentrics*—a publication which might have been subtitled, like Thackeray's *Book of Snobs, By One of Themselves*. As we must have noticed, the appellation of *humorist* was initially applied to an eccentric, rather than to a writer who pointed out the eccentricity. Gradually it shifted from the objective to the subjective mood, and from the passive to the active sense. Samuel Butler is said to have marked the transition, very likely because he was identified with his humoristic creation, Hudibras. Yet when Corbyn Morris brought forth his *Essay towards Fixing the True Standards of Wit, Humour, Raillery, Satire, and Ridicule* in 1744, he took the earlier attitude: *To Which is Added, an Analysis of the Characters of an Humourist, Sir John Falstaff, Sir Roger de Coverly, and Don Quixote.*

As the focus of humor is shifted from actor to spectator, from the individual whose oddities are noted to the writer who is taking note, a more sympathetic relation seems to develop between the two. Ridicule gives way to empathy; the characterization becomes the author's mouthpiece, not his victim; and the author himself becomes a role-player, a practical joker, a collector of hobby-horses. Laurence Sterne is omnipresent—and very far from invisible—throughout *Tristram Shandy.* Edward Lear is the moonstruck protagonist of his own limericks, and Lewis Carroll's nonsense is the looking-glass image of his Oxonian logic. Dickens was notoriously implicated in acting out the lives of his characters through his public readings. Typically, the American humorist has been a monologuist, drawling or misspelling a rustic dialect under a facetious pseudonym. His performance is that of an *eíron*, a self-ironist who dissembles his wit—like Socrates, or like Will Rogers saying "All I know is what I read in the papers," or like the accident-prone anecdotists in *The New Yorker*. (The related case of Falstaff is complicated, in this respect as in so many others. He comes on as an *alazón*, the *eíron's* opposite, the eternal braggart whose boasts will be duly exposed, and hence the cause that wit is in other men. But, being wittier in himself than they are in themselves, he rises above his temporary discomfiture and contrives to outwit them. He is an *eíron* masking as an *alazón*.)

The extraordinary softening that English humor underwent

during the eighteenth century and the Romantic period has been chronicled step by step in a valuable study by Stuart M. Tave, *The Amiable Humorist*. The reservations voiced in Sir Richard Blackmore's *Essay upon Wit* (1716) are among the indications of a collective change from satirical raillery to cheerful benevolence. Socially this can be correlated with the increasing pervasion of middle-class sentimentality. "Between Swift and Sterne," as E. N. Hooker has written, "a mighty chasm occurs." Out of that chasm arise the mollifying concepts of good humor, good nature, innocent mirth, sweet philanthropy, and pathos. Andrew Lang would retrospectively comment that the old-fashioned humor had gone out of English life together with its old-fashioned cruelty. The transformation is graphic when we turn from Hogarth and Gillray to Cruikshank and Phiz. The levelling process had so repressed the originals, and thereby so impoverished the theater, that Hazlitt could believe: "We are deficient in comedy because we are without character in real life." He underestimated the extent to which comedy and character would stage their resurgence in the Dickensian novel; and Dickens, with all his sentimental Victorianism, could draw upon a counter-balancing strain which was pungently Jonsonian. Amiable humor had its heyday in the essays of Charles Lamb, where the writer struck up an intimacy with the reader, to whom he confided his nostalgias and whimsies.

It was William Makepeace Thackeray, in a lecture entitled "Charity and Humour," who expounded what could be taken as the official Victorian formulation. Thackeray's professions of worldly cynicism and his fondness for Augustan pastiche hint that he might have been more at ease among the coffee-house wits in the age of Queen Anne; but his *Lectures on the English Humourists of the Eighteenth Century*, aimed at a nineteenth-century audience, are biographical, moralistic, and by no means nostalgic. An assignment coupling humor with charity would inevitably subjoin other qualities, notably tears, and would indulge the lecturer's penchant for sermonizing. Humorists are "weekday preachers"; Mr. Punch himself "preaches from his booth"; and "Was there ever a better charity sermon preached in the world than Dickens' 'Christmas Carol'?" Thackeray's tone sounds forced whenever he speaks of Dickens, and he must surely do so on this occasion: "What a humor! and what a good humor!" To sum it all up in two monosyllables, "humor is wit and love"—a recipe which Thackeray interjected into the much less charitable context of *Mr. Brown's Letters to his Nephew*. As for the humorist:

> A literary man of the humoristic turn is pretty sure to be of a philanthropic nature, to have a great sensibility, to be easily moved to pain or pleasure, keenly to appreciate the varieties of temper of people round about him, and sympathize in their laughter, love, amusement, tears. Such a man is philanthropic, man-loving by nature, as another is irascible, or red-haired, or six feet high.

If this be a portrait of Dickens—and it is manifestly not a self-portrait—we should have to add that irascibility is as much a part of his humor as philanthropy. But the propensity to overflow the normal limits of definition, and to blur the picture by throwing in extraneous matter, is habitual with our subject, as should by now be evident. It reaches its most transcendent heights when Thomas Carlyle, that virtuoso of overstatement, undertakes to describe the indescribable humor of Jean-Paul Richter:

> . . . it is vast, rude, irregular; often perhaps overstrained and extravagant; yet fundamentally it is genuine humor, the humor of Cervantes and Sterne, and product not of Contempt but Love, not of superficial distortion of natural forms, but of deep and playful sympathy with all forms. It springs not less from the heart than from the head; its result is not laughter, but something far kindlier and better; as it were, the balm which a generous spirit pours over the wounds of life, and which none but a generous spirit can give forth. Such humor is compatible with tenderest and sublimest feelings, or rather it is incompatible with the want of them.

Joe Miller, the name of a long defunct comedian, has survived among his compatriots as a byword for the unblinking fact that jokes get stale. Jean-Paul no longer seems quite so cosmic a genius, and Carlyle has all but dropped out of the syllabus. The tenderness he lovingly dwelt upon has given way to a resurgence of toughness during our more violent century; and the wheel has come full circle, revolving back from amiability to aggressiveness, to a more sharply satirical frame of mind. George Bernard Shaw, though both a wit and a humanitarian, would not have been numbered by Thackeray among "the kind English humorists." Comedy, with Bertolt Brecht or Samuel Beckett or Eugène Ionesco or Harold Pinter, has moved from sympathy to alienation. Absurdity is treated seriously, as indeed it must be when it breaks in on us from all directions and unsettles the presuppositions of daily living. Grotesquerie has come into its own. André Breton, two generations ago, rediscovered the roots of Surrealism in *l'humour noir*; and if the English have not figured prominently among its current exponents, they were its pioneers and Swift was its "veritable initiator," in the testimonial of Breton. Black Humor too confronts us literally, as the power of Afro-American blackness asserts itself in our time. The struggle has not abated as the protean challenger has continued to change his shape. "Trying to define humor," said that dazzling artist Saul Steinberg, in a retrospective interview with Pierre Schneider, "is one of the definitions of humor."

D

THE WAGES OF SATIRE

> It is indeed acting but a poor part in life, to make a business
> of laughing at the follies of others. It is injurious to one's
> self; for there is a great deal more to be gained by soothing and
> praising what men do, than by finding fault with them. It
> may be said of satire, what was said of anger by some
> philosopher, it never pays the service it requires.

This epigraph comes tongue-in-cheek from Hugh Henry
Brackenridge's *Modern Chivalry,* that picaresque novel which—
rather more incisively than the mock-epic effusions of the so-
called Connecticut Wits—scrutinized the American republic in
its formative years. It may well happen that such endeavors fall
on infertile soil. Dickens' first visit hither led him to the impression that "no satirist could breathe this air." Ambrose Bierce
made repeated attempts and embittered complaints before his
ultimate disappearance across the Mexican border. Mark Twain
enacted the paradigmatic role of the muffled satirical genius.

Moss Hart laid down a Broadway definition: "Satire is what closes on Saturday night." Our talented neighbor, Robertson Davies, has drawn a suggestive inference from the slightly more recent Canadian experience: "countries that are not always sure of their own identity are understandably suspicious of satirists." During the present century we Americans have become pretty sure of our identity, for better or for worse, and the attendant complacencies have called forth the increasingly mordant critiques of H. L. Mencken, Sinclair Lewis, John Dos Passos, Nathanael West, and the current generation of Black Humorists. Ours must be among those times and places, like Juvenal's, when it seems difficult not to write satire. When such an impetus gets voiced in protest, there must be at least a hope for some response.

Yet satirists have characteristically spoken of facing a hopeless as well as a thankless task. Earnestly they have reaffirmed the jest of Brackenridge: satire does not pay, it has seldom rewarded the strenuous exertions that have gone into it. "Perhaps," so Dr. Johnson has attested, "neither Pope nor Boileau has made the world much better than he found it." And Swift, in a purported letter from Gulliver to his cousin and editor, Richard Sympson, confided impatiently: "I cannot learn that my book hath produced one single effect according to my intention." Political parties are still riven by factions; lawcourts are still teeming with abuses; men and women go on behaving like Yahoos, in spite of what they might have learned by reading *Gulliver's Travels* during the almost seven months since its publication. As for Voltaire, he rarely mentioned satire without deploring it, regarding it as unwarranted attack and himself as primarily a defender. When it was not *"le poison de la littérature,"* it was *"ce genre funeste, ce métier infâme"*—colluding through that last adjective with everything he detested. His *Mémoire sur la satire* was a counterattack on his detractors. Anticipating Johnson, he asked himself what the satires of Boileau had accomplished, and answered that the results were nugatory even when they were not detrimental to both sides.

For unqualified belief in the power of satire, we should have to turn back—as Robert C. Elliott does in his interesting book of that name—to a primitive state of mind which believed as strongly in curses as in blessings. Seen within its own purview, malediction was a form of tribal magic, and Irish bards could exterminate rats by enunciating the appropriate rhymes. Satirists are like witches who stick pins in the effigies of their enemies. Professor Elliott likewise recalls Archilochus, their Greek prototype, whose avenging iambics reportedly drove his fiancée and her promise-breaking father to suicide. But this was not a supernatural feat, since they had been shamed into acting upon their own volition. Their action did depend on communal standards of conformity, and on the poet's effort to maintain them by scoffing publicly at deviations from them. Satire addresses its appeal to a sense of shame, according to Evelyn Waugh among others. Hence, he would imply, it is devalued in a period as shameless as our own, when writers expose themselves. The most traditional function of poetry has been to dispense praise or blame, *laus et vituperatio*. At the higher level, hymns and dithyrambs celebrated the exemplary virtues of gods and heroes. On the lower plane, the object lessons were cautionary lampoons of meaner subjects. All that Aristotle had to say in the matter was to draw the foregoing distinction.

Sheer invective could be ceremonialized. The flyting, where insults were traded, was a game to be judged by the virtuosity of the rival name-callers. Carnivals, betrothals, and other rites of initiation featured licensed episodes of hazing, charivari, or pasquinade. Satire, as a literary genre, has never been very easy to pin down. Though the Romans—through Quintilian—claimed it as their own, they could only define it as a mixed mode, with a Hellenic precedent in Menippus, whose lost medleys would ripen into the dialogues of Lucian and Erasmus. Insofar as it gives vent to denunciation and diatribe, satire has much in common with the prophet's jeremiad or the statesman's philippic. It often coincides with pamphleteering, as in Junius or Courier, not to mention Swift. Habitually stepping into controversy, its implicit war-cries are *"J'accuse!"* and "I will be heard!" But it must be distinguished from such plaints as that of *Piers Plowman* or of Harriet Beecher Stowe by its closer dependence on comic techniques. Significantly, though the verb *to satirize* is of Latin origin, its synonym in Greek was *kōmoidein*: literally, *to comedize*. Yet Milton relates it to the tragic impulse, and Brecht to the epic key. Comedy always has a satiric potential, usually balanced—and in Shakespeare's case overbalanced—by its purely festive or romantic element.

When comedy becomes more purposeful than playful, then it is satire. The most direct and powerful conjunction of the two has been the Old Comedy of Aristophanes, inasmuch as it held an institutional place in the city-state of Athens. This has frequently been compared to a municipal pillory, since it represented actual personages and subjected them to unsparing mockeries. Witness its recurrent target, Cleon, the war-mongering demagogue. Aristophanes, censured for one such allusion, forbidden to let his actor use an identifying mask, sarcastically mimicked a recognizable quirk of Cleon's speech in *The Knights*. But the Peloponnesian War continued nonetheless, meting out ironic retribution to the bellicose politician—now a general—by killing him off. Aristophanes could boast of having dared to oppose civic policy, but not of having affected it. Though the plays were popular, "the people were far from being guided by the same sentiments in the theater and in the elections," as the commentator Maurice Croiset remarked. It is a disquieting afterthought that Aristophanes may have exerted more impact when he ridiculed Socrates in *The Clouds*. That charlatanical figure was presented as the polar opposite of its living model. Whereas the original embodied the self-deprecating wisdom of the *eíron*, the caricature exhibited the specious pretensions to knowledge of an *alazón*.

Pedantry forever invites and merits derision, but scoffers are sometimes too ready to suspect it in the techniques of empirical science. Swift would burlesque the Royal Society, in his Academy of Lagado, with experiments as idiotic as those performed in Aristophanes' think-tank, the Phrontistérion. Both satirists there-

by lay themselves open to a possible charge of anti-intellec-
tualism, and there is more than a tinge of the philistine in
Aristophanes' campaign against the newfangled notions of Euripides. We are aware that the animus of *The Clouds* was not *ad
hominem*; Aristophanes converses warmly with the real Socrates
in that happiest of conversations, Plato's *Symposium*. The veritable target, dialectically dramatized in the agon between personifications of right and wrong, was the demoralizing influence of
the Sophists; and Plato sets on record, in his *Protagoras*, a Socrates who is the sharpest critic of the Sophists' school of thought.
Lessing has argued that the spectators recognized this difference
when Socrates attended the performance and stood up, that
Aristophanes—while portraying a "dangerous Sophist"—had
merely misappropriated the proper name. The resulting confusion is like what happens with many a *roman à clef*, when the sins
of a fictitious character are visited upon his human semblance.
Aristophanes' strictures contributed to the danger that menaced
Socrates, if not to his subsequent execution.

That was a Pyrrhic victory for satire. If the Aristophanic in-
quest proved ineffectual with the slippery Cleon, it succeeded in
tainting the most virtuous of philosophers. Since the playwright
was not an ideologue, his ideas were not especially consistent or
systematic. Yet he had his positive values; he was an inveterate
laudator temporis acti; and he reckoned with contemporary tur-
bulence by the more peaceable criteria of the noble old Athenian
democracy. Every satirist, negative though he may sound, must
project his guided missiles from a launching-pad of belief. Carlyle's nagging was grounded in his hero-worship; Tacitus, de-
nouncing the Roman emperors, idealized the Germanic chiefs.
Dos Passos, testifying for himself and other realists who were
disillusioned idealists, has written: "Maybe it is that the satirist is
so full of the possibilities of humankind in general that he tends
to draw a dark and garish picture when he tries to depict people as
they are at any particular moment." In terms of Aristotelian
logic, we must look for the enthymeme: the unexpressed principle, the unstated premise of an abridged syllogism, the affirma-

tive conviction that lies behind the pejorative demonstration. To
the extent that this can be taken for granted and shared with his
public, it is an advantage for the satirist to speak from a conser-
vative position, to be confirmed by a status quo.

Not that he is necessarily bound to become a spokesman for
the Tories on any given issue. (Even Swift started out as a Whig,
choosing panegyric as his earliest strain, and transposing it to
satire after he had experienced worldly disappointments and ideological tergiversations.) But we do encounter a problem here
which was formulated rather apologetically by Lionel Trilling in
his well-known essay on "The Liberal Imagination," with its
large concessions to literary conservatism. We need not ignore
the converse attitudes summed up by Van Wyck Brooks, when
he declared that the heart of the American writer was on the left.
Yet the satirist must convince his audience that, when something
is rotten or someone goes astray, there has been a departure from
a certain ethos. It is simpler for him when the norms of that ethos
have already been accepted by convention. Otherwise, it becomes a part of his job to inculcate those norms—in other words,
to preach to the unconverted. He must be hortatory before he can
wax sardonic, like Bernard Shaw in the prefaces to his plays.
Satire is perceived as a radical force in the sense that it disturbs
the peace, that it undermines the vested interests, which remain
poised to resist and to strike back. It is not a question of politics
but of human nature that we find it so much easier to reject
novelties than we do to criticize traditions.

And, since not every change is an improvement, it serves little
purpose to align our satirists along a spectrum extending from
progressive to reactionary. All of them are iconoclasts in the most
literal sense, in that they have dedicated themselves to the breaking of images. "The end of satire is reformation," affirmed Defoe. Yet reformation can look backward as well as forward. The
satirist is an *ipso facto* moralist, promoting the good by excoriat-
ing the bad according to his lights. Albeit Shaw was more obviously an iconoclast or reformer, Aristophanes, as an avowed
traditionalist, lamented the passing of a notably democratic re-

gime. Faced with the new constraints, he underwent the straitening transition from Old to Middle Comedy in his last two surviving plays. He could draw upon his own rich vein of fantasy, in avoiding the hazards of topical argument. But it was a crucial loss to omit the *parábasis*, that choric interlude which gave voice directly to the socio-political views of the dramatist. By the time of Menander, New Comedy had withdrawn its gaze from public to private life, and had standardized its dramatis personae by using stock types instead of libelling extant personalities. Continuing through Plautus and Terence via the Commedia dell' Arte to an apogee in Molière, the comic stage concentrated more on general traits than on individual foibles.

Fielding would make the conventional disclaimer that fends off lawsuits based on non-coincidental resemblances: "I declare here once for all, I describe not men but manners, not an individual but a species." Molière's apologist, in his self-defense, had explained: *"Son dessin est de peindre les moeurs sans vouloir toucher les personnes."* At a highly serious moment, while defending *Tartuffe*, Molière added a moral emphasis: *"Le devoir de la comédie est de corriger les hommes en les divertissant."* Correction, as administered through schooling, involved castigation. *"Castigat ridendo mores"* was the Latin motto of the leading Franco-Italian Harlequin, one of Molière's theatrical rivals, and the schoolmaster's rod or scourge was the satirist's emblem. Swift retained his habitual doubts about its effectiveness: "Now, if I know anything of mankind, these gentlemen might very well spare their reproof and correction; for there is not, through all nature, another so callous and insensible a member as the world's posteriors, whether you apply to it the toe or the birch." Disclaiming "the satirical itch" in his preface to A *Tale of a Tub*, and arguing that panegyric is more invidious than satire, he points out that the Athenians could rail against their fellow citizens, whereas the English—though personally protected by libel laws—were free to level their "utmost rhetoric against mankind."

But he went on, in opening his preface to *The Battle of the Books*, to suggest that such rhetoric was lost upon the obtuse and impervious readers: "Satire is a sort of *glass*, wherein beholders do generally discover everybody's face but their own; which is the chief reason for that kind of reception it meets in the world, and that so very few are offended with it." The metaphor of comedy as a mirror of human behavior ("*speculum consuetudinis*") can be traced as far back as Cicero, and since the Middle Ages had been coupled with the moralistic hope that the viewer might be prompted to mend his reflected conduct. The fullest exposition of this idea is the Induction to Ben Jonson's *Every Man out of his Humor*, the first of those three self-styled "comical satires" which unsuccessfully illustrated his critical and clinical theories. It is probable that Shakespeare was glancing obliquely at Jonson's saturnine spokesman, when his melancholy Jaques offered to "Cleanse the whole body of th'infected world, / If they will patiently receive my medicine." Here the image for the satirical process is not a scourge but a purge, not a punitive but a therapeutic occasion. The meaning is underscored by the vulgar pun between *Jaques* and *jakes* (the Elizabethan word for privy), which predicates a close and concrete equivalent for the catharsis of tragedy.

Pope would consider the punishment to be part of a treatment in ethical therapy. "Satire . . . ," for him, "heals with morals what it hurts with wit." For Samuel Johnson, on the other hand, such wounds found no cures. In his *Rambler* allegory on wit and learning, he opines: "Wit, cohabiting with Malice, had a son named Satyr, who followed him, carrying a quiver filled with poisoned arrows, which, where they once drew blood, could by no skill be extracted." By conflating satire with the Greek satyr-play, through the usual false etymology, Johnson personified it as a sort of Cupid in reverse. Hence he tended to balk at it, as W. J. Bate has shown, despite his formidable powers as a moralist. Wits of the previous generation had been more ironically tough-minded in their prescriptions for social ills: Defoe in suggesting genocide as a remedy for dissent, Swift in proposing cannibalism as an antidote to famine. It is generally agreed that English satire enjoyed its heyday during the first half of the eighteenth century;

it declined as, with the emergence of mere sentimental and romantic touchstones, wit deserted malice and mellowed into humor. Addison's *Spectator* was a precursor here, anticipating Johnson with caveats against satire's poisonous darts. In the hands of Pope—who, for all his *Imitations of Horace*, took a sternly Juvenalian stance—it remained a "sacred weapon."

Far from professing to be a respecter of persons, Pope strove for their fullest exposure. When his interlocutor enjoins him to "spare the person and expose the vice," he completes the couplet by retorting: "How, sir? not damn the sharper but the dice?" Some of his victims deserve better from posterity than to have survived as mere footnotes to pungent epithets and virulent epigrams. (This is incidentally true of Thomas Shadwell, who wrote better comedies than Dryden, which have been disregarded because of *MacFlecknoe*.) But most of Pope's moth-like dunces were unworthy of the pains he took to break them upon his massive wheel (like the forgotten butts of Goethe's and Schiller's *Xenien*). As an ambitious monument to dullness, *The Dunciad* was ineluctably destined to display the attribute it celebrates. Moreover, a satiric undertaking which flails about so widely is subject to imputations that the author must be a disappointed and angry man seeking personal vengeance, wielding what Browning described in *Aristophanes' Apology* as "the comic weapon . . . , hate." Both Juvenal and Swift after him expressly acknowledged having been motivated by indignation, which can be either mean or exalted, depending upon the provocation. Swift discerned "two ends that men propose in writing satire": one, "private satisfaction"; the other, and more altruistic, "public spirit"—or, to rephrase, one revenge and the other reform.

The former may achieve its sublimation in the latter, when revenge is transposed into reform by a Swift. With a Wyndham Lewis, so jealously begrudging the recognition accorded to some of his more gifted contemporaries, the satirist becomes a common scold whose competitive motives are suspect. With certain other temperaments, like that of Thomas Nashe, he engages in satire for its own sake, animated by sheer polemical exuberance.

Its object, for an Aretino, is no more than blackmail. If poets are unacknowledged legislators, satirists may be self-appointed arbiters of morals. Often constrained to publish anonymously or under a pseudonym, they are adept and protean at establishing a persona, which may range from the urbane Horatian conversationalist to the impressionable Voltairean *ingénu*. They are likewise so prone to distort or exaggerate that their proffered mirror-images go unrecognized by many of their beholders. When, if ever, can we be sure that the weapon has hit its mark, or—to put it more constructively—that the medicine has effected a cure? Joseph Hall, who proclaimed himself the first English satirist, divided his experimental productions into two categories: "toothless" and "biting" satires. The first were by definition impotent, if not a contradiction in terms. The second constituted just enough of an irritant to get the biter bitten. In 1599, by a decree of the Anglican Church, all such works were banned and condemned to be burned.

The sacred weapon could turn out to be a boomerang. Satire runs a continual risk from the backlash of suppression. Furthermore, as Isacc D'Israeli noted, "Satirists, if they escape the scourge of the law, have reason to dread the cane of the satirized." Thus Dryden was beaten up by the hired thugs of the Earl of Rochester, as was Voltaire in his turn by those of the Chevalier de Rohan—and then, when the victim protested, he was victimized further by imprisonment in the Bastille. Juvenal had been exiled by the Emperor Domitian; so would Victor Hugo be under Louis Napoleon. Swift seems to have been denied a bishopric because Queen Anne was too literal-minded a reader to follow the religious parable in *A Tale of a Tub*. Defoe's heavily ironic pamphlet, *The Shortest Way with the Dissenters*, misfired with still more adverse consequences to the author, who was pilloried for seditious libel. Thereupon, cheered by the people who witnessed his official disgrace, he wrote an unregenerate "Hymn to the Pillory," along with a *Brief Explanation* of his intentions: "If any man take the pains seriously to reflect upon the contents, the nature of the thing, and the manner of the style, it seems impossible to imagine that it should pass for anything but an irony." Yet, taken at face value, it had been denounced by fellow Dissenters, while being hailed by the Tory extremists whose bigotry it mocked.

Benjamin Franklin used a similar tactic in *An Edict of the King of Prussia*, where the ironic pretense was that Germany would exact the same demands from Britain that the British were exacting from the American colonies. Resident in England when it appeared, Franklin was amused to watch English friends being all but taken in by the hoax before recognizing its critical thrust. Irony is so ambiguous a device—not to say two-edged—that it is more than ordinarily susceptible to miscarriage, since it aims at levels of perception beyond the ironist's control. Socrates was both its incarnation and its martyr. Lord Northcliffe is reported to have forbidden its use in his newspapers, on the grounds that it misled too many readers and that it was resented by most of those who understood. The Earl of Shaftesbury, who had more confidence in the reading public of his day, had been willing to let it judge for itself. Satire was a corrective for him, "a remedy against vice" and a vehicle of poetic justice. From the postulate, "Nothing is ridiculous except what is deformed," he reasoned that "a subject which could not bear raillery was suspicious," and came to the reverberating conclusion that ridicule was the test of truth, "which may bear all lights." This accords with President Truman's assertion that a demagogue cannot stand laughter (evidently he was not thinking of Cleon). But it does not fit in very well with the libellous put-down of the truth-seeker, Socrates.

Tested in the light of history, the Shaftesbury-Truman doctrine seems to have been over-optimistic. Hitler's demogogy was incomparably worse than Cleon's; and it evoked a folklore of underground humor among his victims; but that could hardly have resulted in dismissing him as a laughingstock. Conversely, the grotesque cartoons in Nazi publications like *Der Stürmer* made effective propaganda for anti-Semitism. Gibes could hurt the underdog if not the top dog, who was insulated from the stings of defamation. Today, on the other side of the Iron Curtain, jokes against the government abound. One of the oldest and most familiar might be reiterated as an archetype. A comrade asks, "What is the difference between capitalism and socialism?" To which his more sophisticated comrade replies: "Capitalism is the exploitation of man by man, and socialism is the reverse." This not only neutralizes the purport of the basic Marxian antithesis; it parodies the doctrinaire tone of a communist catechism. It could not be more subversive, yet it has propagated, and seems to have had no practical effect. Perhaps it may have functioned, like *samizdat*, to register alternative possibilities under repressive conditions. But such muted disgruntlement might also have acted as a safety-valve to let off steam from a dissidence which could otherwise have exploded. A joke, by Freud's account, is a way of sublimating hostility.

Under these clandestine circumstances, the fight is for survival rather than conquest; the commitment is to keep an ethic of humanity alive against monstrous odds. Since totalitarian regimes have trouble in living up to their own propaganda, they offer a standing incitement to satire, which of course they can ill afford. It broke out in Soviet Russia, while permitted, through such ironists as Mikhail Bulgakov, Valentin Kataev, and Ilf-and-Petrov; and, though now suppressed in the mother country, is exported by Andrei Siniavsky and Vladimir Voinovich. Yet their major theme, the bunglings of the bureaucracy, had deep roots in the Tsarist tradition, and could hark back to Gogol as its past master. Curiously enough, the work of literature that influenced the course of Russian empire most decisively, was composed by the least didactic of its great novelists, Turgenev's *Sketches of a Sportsman*. This has been credited with playing a part in the demise of serfdom, *mutatis mutandis*, comparable to that of the heavier-handed *Uncle Tom's Cabin* in the abolition of slavery. Doubtless neither could have been more than a contributing factor, publicizing a historical movement which battled on many different fronts. Dickens, as George Orwell and Humphry House have demonstrated, was not so much a social reformer as he was a humanitarian publicist. Did Cervantes smile Spain's chivalry away, as Byron regretted, or did he smile to see it crumble away? Questions regarding the efficacy of satire, as a means of signalizing and attaining definite objectives, are more readily met when they involve particular cases rather than widespread causes. Voltaire's crowded and prolonged career was a sequence of crusades against the despotic and superstitious adversaries that he lumped together under his militant slogan, *"Ecrasez l'infâme!"* His successes could be measured by the campaigns he waged and won on behalf of those condemned to death for heresy: the rehabilitation of Calas (unhappily posthumous), the actual deliverance of Sirven. He could not have done this without recourse to "public opinion"—a concept he was early in formulating. Gibbon would introduce it into English not long afterward, and Jefferson would duly apply it in an American context. Voltaire's strategy was posited upon the growth of a literate middle-class audience, and consequently a greater concern for its sympathies and potential support. Swift, among his devastating Houynhnhyms, had disparaged relativistic opinion in favor of absolute reason; but that was not held up to men as an attainable ideal. He had previously triumphed as a pamphleteer, fabricating his Bickerstaff predictions to confound the quack almanacs of John Partridge. "The Dean did by his pen defeat / An infamous destructive cheat," Swift was entitled to crow in self-eulogy, after his *Drapier's Letters* had deflated the monopolistic coinage of William Wood.

Facetiously, a year before he published *Gulliver's Travels,* Swift told a friend that it would "mend the world." He was speaking more seriously in a better-known letter to Pope, when he announced a countervailing intention "to vex the world rather than divert it." There too he disclosed the "great foundation of misanthropy" on which he was constructing his masterpiece: "I have ever hated all nations, professions, and communities, and all my love is toward individuals . . . But principally I detest that animal called man, although I heartily love John, Peter, Thomas, and so forth." Satire at that stage moves beyond revenges and reforms, well beyond individuals or institutions, toward a sweeping overview of the human condition. Nothing is so broadening for our perspectives as travel, and it is no accident that so many

satires—from Lucian's *True History* onward—are *voyages imag-
inaires*. These detach us from our culture-bound scales of mea-
surement, whether by diminution in Lilliput (whose inhabitants
are one-twelfth the size of man) or by magnification in Brob-
dingnag (where the natives are twelve times larger than ordinary
humans). Voltaire's interplanetary science-fiction, with *Micro-
mégas*, comprises both extremes in the very name. Whether a
giant is less absurd than a dwarf hinges upon the observer's
height. Swift was even-handed in discerning the frailties or
blemishes of each—unlike Rabelais, whose gigantism was much
more high-spirited.

Reduction is the more habitual method of imposing absurdity.
Orwell reduces society to the rusticity of a beast-fable in *Animal
Farm*, and to the regimentation of a dystopia in *1984*. Yet belit-
tlement can scarcely be envisioned without a corresponding enlargement in the point of view. This might be termed—in the
wake of Bertolt Brecht—a V*erfremdungseffekt*, a deliberate alienation or psychic distancing. Though satirists can all too easily get
enmeshed in petty immediacies, the greatest satires are those that
take the longest views: *Gulliver's Travels* preeminently, along
with the closely affiliated *contes philosophiques* of Voltaire. The
Frenchman, in spite of contemporaneous prestige as a philoso-
pher, historian, poet, and dramatist, survives for us largely because of these *bagatelles*. Though they rapidly and cynically
venture across the world and into outer space, they return to the
darkest and deepest problems of mankind, not to solve them but
to sustain the episodic inquiry. *Candide*, which so rigorously tests
and so critically undermines the philosophy of its subtitle, *L'Op-
timisme*, is concerned with nothing less than theodicy: cosmic
justice, the nature of evil, the preoccupation of *King Lear*. *Zadig*
arrives at a conventional happy ending after an extremely gloomy
chapter in which a hermit, who turns into an angel, urges the
hero to accept a grossly malfunctioning universe. The hero's last
word, interrupted by the flight of the angel, is "*Mais*—." The
satirist's vocation might be succinctly epitomized in that suspended monosyllable: "But—."

Index

207